Healing Your
Inner Child

---

7 Beginner Steps to Reparent and Free
Yourself from Past Childhood Trauma,
Heal Deep Wounds, and Live Life
Authentically

Caldwell Ramsey

Healing your Inner Child, by Caldwell Ramsey ©2022
ISBN: 9798840605424

TABLE OF CONTENTS

Just For You

A Free Gift For All My Readers

Inner Child Healing Workbook with complementary tools for your healing journey. Visit my website:

www.CaldwellRamseybooks.com

INTRODUCTION

"Nothing is permanent."

Dalai Lama

Have you ever wondered why you can't find healing, no matter what you do? Or why you feel stuck with internal pain that just won't go away? Maybe you've tried to change the cycle, escape the loop, but you still fall back on old ways. Maybe you've tried therapy, but even that hasn't helped. The answers to the questions you're asking about your hurt and pain are inside you. The cry you feel from deep down in your heart comes from the wounded child within. *Your inner child.*

Now you may be wondering, what is an inner child and why is mine wounded? As little ones, we've all experienced difficult times. More than two-thirds of children report that they've experienced trauma before the age of sixteen[1]. Trauma gets carried from childhood into adulthood through our inner child. We're afraid of experiencing the pain again, so we bury it. We send this child to a deep, dark place inside and stay as far away from it as possible. Unfortunately, running (and hiding) doesn't end the suffering, it only prolongs it. Your inner child yearns for healing and validation. *The little you* within you – within your psyche, that is – longs to be recognized by you.

To truly heal on a deep cellular level, we need to learn to love the little person inside of us. We need to love the little one that didn't receive love the way they should have, that didn't feel safe and secure on the dark nights. The little one that's been living with the fear that they'll never be good enough. We need to pull that child in, embrace them and tell them, "It's okay now. You took on so much that was not yours to bear, but I am here now." Only then, will we become the love for ourselves that we never had.

---

[1] https://www.samhsa.gov/child-trauma/understanding-child-trauma#:~:text=At%20least%201%20in%207,for%20physical%20assault-related%20injuries

I grew up with parents who were workaholics. They were in a toxic marriage, and although they meant me no harm, my home-life situation left me with open wounds that I struggled with into my adult life. I have come to realize that children don't get traumatized because they get hurt; they get traumatized when they're left all alone with that hurt. It took me a long time to realize that what I needed was inner child healing. I have been prescribed multiple antidepressants throughout my life, joined life coaching sessions, read all the self-help books, and even seen a therapist or two. These tools made me feel better for a little while, but eventually, the pain crept back, and I returned to my old ways of thinking and living, which made me miserable. It was like putting a band-aid on a bullet wound.

It was only when I attended a sound therapy session (as a favor to a friend who was completing her training) that I came across the term *inner child healing.* Out of desperation, I looked further into it and realized that my inner child was wounded. I began my healing journey, and it changed my life. Through reparenting and connecting with my inner child using the holistic methods we're going to discuss in this book, I was finally able to free myself from my past trauma and awaken my authentic self.

The purpose of this book is to guide you through finding freedom and inner sanctity. You deserve relief. You deserve to have that weight lifted off your chest. You deserve to follow your path, find peace where there was once pain, and walk your *own self* towards healing. Helping you understand the source of your pain and how to heal yourself matters deeply to me.

Together, we will discover what an inner child is and how to determine if your inner child is wounded. We will uncover the importance of being open to healing and the different holistic methods to start your healing process. I will help you through mindfulness, communication, self-love, breathwork, meditation, and setting healthy boundaries.

Here are a few topics we will be talking about:

1. A Wounded Inner Child

You may have heard the term inner child before, or it may be completely new to you. This journey will begin by discovering what the wounded inner child is and determining if your inner child is suffering.

2. Trauma In the Brain

Childhood trauma can lead to an adult living in survival mode. The trauma you have experienced as a child often affects you later in life, even though you may not be conscious of it. Understanding how your trauma has affected you is one of the first steps to healing.

3. Empowered Healing

The trauma may not be your fault, but the healing is your responsibility. The fact that you've chosen this book is proof that you want to heal. It is important to have an open heart and open mind when it comes to your healing journey.

4. Inner Child Healing

Once you recognize who your inner child is, the next step is to understand inner child healing and how to set yourself free from the anguish you've been feeling.

5. Reparenting

Reparenting is one of the most important steps when it comes to healing. You need to redo the parenting process on yourself in order to heal your inner child.

6. The Energy of Mindfulness

It is important to understand the energy of mindfulness while on your healing journey. Having the right mindset and being mindful of your inner child are very important.

7. Validate and Notice Yourself

Another essential part of the healing process is noticing and validating yourself. You need to take care of your present self so that while you're doing the inner child work, you're not neglecting the here and now.

8. Personal Healing: Self Love & Self Care

Part of noticing and validating yourself is observing your feelings and including some extra self-love and self-care into your life.

9. Breathwork

Breathing is so important, yet it's something we don't do enough of. Discovering how to do breathwork and incorporating specific breathing practices for inner child healing will make a world of difference in your healing journey.

10. Meditation Healing

When your mind is calm, powerful things can happen and you will find deep healing. Learning how to meditate for inner child healing is another essential practice to help you along your journey.

11. The Mighty Pen

Journaling and writing letters to yourself allows you to direct your focus on your innermost thoughts and feelings. It is a chance to express yourself in a vulnerable way to facilitate your inner child's healing.

12. Back To The Drawing Board

A great activity for inner child healing is drawing. It may sound trivia, but art (yes, even stick figure drawings) can permeate the very deepest part of you, where no words exist.

13. Inner Child Communication

Communication is key. I'm sure you've heard that one hundred times, but learning to communicate what your inner child is feeling versus what your adult self is feeling is essential to this journey. It is also okay to see a professional if you aren't coping and the trauma is too deep. While a big part of your healing has to come from you, there is nothing wrong with finding someone to help you make sense of it all, especially if it's someone who works with inner child healing.

I wrote this book because I believe that healing your inner child's pain is the key to transforming your anger, sadness, and fear. I know what it's like to feel lost, with no idea where to start the healing or why you're even hurting in the first place. Childhood trauma is often overlooked when adults are trying to heal themselves. I want to communicate the importance of being mindful of your inner child and constantly working on the relationship with them to achieve harmony within your life.

The methods in this book have helped me with my own healing journey. They have allowed me to thrive in my personal development and have opened up a gateway of possibilities in my life. All I want is the same for you. I want you to reconnect with your inner child, to find blissful contentment after the years of agony. As traumatized children, we always dream that someone will come and save us. I know I never dreamed that it would, in fact, be myself as an adult. Through this book and the knowledge and passion I want to share with you, my goal is to help *you* become the savior for your *inner child.*

CHAPTER ONE: A WOUNDED INNER CHILD

"The wound is the place where the Light enters you."

~ Rumi

Everyone has an inner child that reminds us of our playful spirit and carefree days. But many times as children, we are mentally and emotionally wounded, mistreated, and ignored, leaving us with scars that never heal. Our inner child gets stuck and doesn't grow and develop with us as we age. This leads to difficulties later on in life that can leave us feeling miserable. The first step to healing on a deep, cellular level is to acknowledge who your inner child is and understand that they're wounded. By choosing this book, you've chosen to take action towards altering your life for the better. To fully heal yourself as an adult, you need to embrace the child within and work towards healing their wounds.

What is an Inner Child?

We were all once children, but now even though we are adults, we still have a child residing within us. However, most adults are completely unaware of this, and it is for this reason that we experience so many emotional, spiritual, and interpersonal challenges throughout our lives. As we progress along our journey from little-one to big-one, we are constantly told to put "childish" things aside and grow up. From a physiological viewpoint, adulthood is not merely aging. Rather, being an adult is all about the three A's; *acknowledging, accepting*, and taking *accountability* for loving and parenting our inner child. The problem is that as we grow up, we're taught that our inner child, which represents our child-like capacity for curiosity, joy, wonderment, innocence, playfulness, and empathy, must be silenced, suppressed, or even destroyed. Our inner child encompasses all of the positive qualities, but it also includes our accumulated childhood worry, fear, anger, pain, and trauma. Grown-ups are convinced that they need to outgrow their child-like ways to function optimally in the adult world, but this is far from the truth. All that ends up happening is we are left with so much suppressed emotional baggage and buried trauma and have no idea why or where it's coming from.

Although our inner child is not physical or tangible, it is part of our deep subconscious. It has been soaking up information way before it was even able to process what was actually going on. Our inner child is always present, always absorbing. The inner child is the one that remembers the sweet smell of grandma's cookies on a Sunday morning and how comforting her hugs were. The inner child remembers the feeling of their heart bursting with joy when their parents looked at them with pride. The inner child remembers how special they used to feel when they were invited to a party. The inner child remembers the feeling of being chosen first for a team and the confidence that came with it. However, the inner child also remembers what it was like to be chosen last. The inner child remembers their dad forgetting their birthday. The inner child remembers kids throwing paper at them and calling them horrible names in class. The inner child remembers the fights between their parents over money and being sent to their room which left them thinking it was all their fault. The inner child remembers feeling stupid after a teacher scoffed at them for asking a "silly" question. The inner child never goes away. They are always there, wrapped in other experiences, wrapped by adolescence, then youth, then by adulthood, and then by old age. But the inner child is ever-present until the day we die.

As adults who have tried to run away from their inner child (or at least the feeling of pain inside), we are still being subconsciously influenced by the child inside us. For many grown-ups, it is not actually our "adult mind" that is in control of the direction of our lives, but rather the emotionally wounded little one dwelling in our adult bodies. It is an angry, scared, and upset little child making the decisions. Because most of us are unaware of our inner child, we end up with self-destructive tendencies, aggressive behavior, commitment issues, fear of abandonment, and even Peter Pan syndrome, which is irresponsibility and angry refusal to be an adult. If you find yourself in a stagnant place in life, your inner child is likely screaming for attention. Situations where you feel stuck can look like challenges in parenting, difficulties at work or preserving love, setting boundaries, or developing relationships.

The dilemma that comes with adults who have wounded inner children is that children are not able to have a career, a mature relationship, or an independent life. Can you imagine two nine-year-olds trying to engage in a serious relationship or deal with conflict in a professional manner? It simply doesn't work, and to some degree, that is exactly what is happening with every adult who has fallen out of touch with their inner child. And then we wonder why we self-sabotage, why our relationships fail, or why we constantly feel anxious, inferior, insecure, and alone. How else would a little child feel in the same situation, without proper love, support, care, or protection? There are so many wounded children living in grown bodies, mimicking adult lives. This is a confusing state of being to live in, so many adults turn to psychotherapy and medication. Being detached from our inner child is far more common than many people realize, and the solution is also easier (not without work, but once you're aware of the problem, you can make the changes) than people think. Our inner child continually communicates with us; we just need to learn to listen.

Common Ways Children Are Neglected

The little ones inside of us hold all of our memories and emotions, positive and negative. Our inner child absorbs the kind words of strangers, the praise from our parents, the pride we felt when we were good at something, and the memories of feeling safe and secure. However, our inner child also absorbs the negative and toxic words and actions of those who were supposed to protect us and give us love. Once wounded, our inner child is negatively affected, which holds great power over who we are as adults.

All children deserve love, security, and safety, and that is more than just in the physical sense. Children deserve to feel protected and cared for on an emotional and spiritual level as well. When a child's needs are fulfilled, they feel secure, but when they are not met, it destroys their sense of safety and leaves them feeling alone, hypervigilant, and afraid. When a child feels repeatedly endangered, their psyche becomes so painfully wounded, and we, as adults, unknowingly try to repress it, but those feelings still linger. It's not only actions that hurt children; words cut like a sword and cause damage on a deeper level. Sometimes the words don't even have to be direct; the damage could result from parents not allowing a child to have an opinion, punishing them for speaking up, or not allowing them to display strong emotions. Children can be wounded when spontaneity is discouraged, or they're not allowed to play and have fun.

Here are three common ways children are made to feel unsafe:

1. Physically

Physical nourishment and security are basic human needs. Children deserve to have these needs met by their caregivers. Sometimes, these basic human rights are lacking, and the child's needs are violated. Physical neglect also refers to more than just food and shelter; it means that the child is exposed to physical or sexual abuse. The tragic results of physical neglect are:

- Self-harm
- Eating disorders
- Addictions
- Low self-esteem
- Aggression and violent behavior
- Sexual dysfunctions

2. Emotionally

Emotional mistreatment means the parents or caregiver neglected the child's needs for love, support, and respect. A child can suffer from emotional neglect when their caregivers don't pay enough attention to them or condemn any emotional expression the child may show. The outcomes from emotional neglect are dire once the child is grown up:

- Anxiety

- Depression

- Low self-worth

- Ignoring emotional needs

- Repressing emotions

- Avoiding emotional closeness and intimacy
- Always questioning the love people show

3. Psychological

This form of neglect is often overlooked and occurs when the child's parents or caregiver fails to be attentive, nurture, and embrace the child for who they are. Psychological neglect includes gaslighting, bullying, teasing, yelling, insults, ridiculing, making threats, and not respecting privacy. The terrible symptoms of psychological neglect are:

- Deep anger
- Addictions
- Neurosis
- Physical and psychological illnesses
- Low self-esteem
- Inability to show self-love
- Lack of respect
- Difficulty maintaining relationships

The Wounded Inner Child

We carry much of our horrible childhood trauma into adulthood because we never really matured into adults. We are basically children who have adapted and are taking on a set of behaviors to protect the wounded inner child. We prefer not to feel the pain of past childhood trauma, so we bury those memories and run far away from them. However, when those memories resurface, we feel like we cannot deal with them, and we deflect them back into the deepest part of our subconscious minds. As a result, our inner child is stifled. If we are unable to reach the little one inside of us, we may never get to heal ourselves. We have to find a way to reach our inner child and make them feel safe and protected again. We have to move past our fear of experiencing pain and address the wound within; that is the only way to true healing.

No matter how much we run or hide behind a smile, there is still a scared child within us. Our inner child affects everything in our lives. They create our fears, insecurities, and self-hatred, damaging our relationships and, ultimately, our life. The wounded child is you and me, and we need to extend a hand to them so that we can recognize, resolve and transform the energy of their suffering. We need to embrace the little one inside of us – exactly as they are – despite their fear and anger for being abandoned for so long.

We need to approach the situation from an adult state of mindfulness and understanding and let our inner child know that it's safe for them to come out from under the bed. As adults who want to heal, the time for running is over. We need to have the courage to do the necessary work to free ourselves from our pain. We need to bring healing to the wounded child within to transform ourselves. When we become aware of our inner child, we can make them a part of our everyday life again. Acknowledging that the child within us is wounded, crying out for help, and taking a step towards reconnecting with them can end the suffering that may have persisted over generations.

Signs you have a wounded inner child

As children, we couldn't meet our own needs. When we experienced trauma, no matter how small it was, we didn't always have the emotional tools to process it. Inevitably, we ended up carrying emotional and psychological wounds that now affect our relationships, health, and career. Emotional wounds that didn't heal correctly or that remain open lead to the development of unhealthy behaviors. Recognizing the signs of your wounded inner child is essential to beginning inner child healing.

Below are some signs that you have a wounded inner child:

- In the deepest parts of me, I feel like there is something very wrong with me.

- I experience immense anxiety whenever thinking about doing something new.

- I feel like a rebel or a misfit. I feel more alive when I'm in conflict with other people.

- I am a people-pleaser, and I tend to lack a strong identity.

- I am inclined to hoard things and have difficulty letting go.

- I feel guilty when standing up for myself.

- I often feel inadequate and "not good enough" as a person.

- I am driven to always be an A+ super-achiever. I put pressure on myself to excel.

- I constantly criticize myself for being inadequate and unworthy.

- I am rigid and a perfectionist.

- I have trouble starting or finishing things.

- I am ashamed of expressing strong emotions like sadness or anger.

- I seldom get mad, but when I do, I become rageful.

- I tend to have sex when I don't want to.

- I am ashamed of my bodily functions.

- I have a hard time trusting anyone, including myself.

- I am an addict or have been addicted to something in the past.

- I avoid conflict at every chance possible.

- I am afraid of people and tend to avoid them.

- I have social anxiety.

- I feel more responsible for other people than for myself.

- I have never felt close to my mother or father.

- My deepest fear is being abandoned, and I'll do anything to cling to a relationship.

- I feel guilty for setting boundaries.

- I struggle to say "no."

If you resonate with many (not necessarily all) of the above items, you likely have a wounded inner child, and it's time to reconnect with the little one inside of you.

If you aren't sure where to start, a helpful way to access the fragmented parts of yourself and discover wounds from your childhood can be by creating a timeline. The beginning of the timeline is when you were born and the end is today, right now. Create a quiet, safe place, step into the time machine and go back to your first memories as close as possible to your starting point – birth. Look back and try to remember details like your age, what was happening around you, and the feelings you felt. Write them all down in order along your timeline leading up to here and now. This way you can really pinpoint the age and trauma of your inner child to better connect with and heal them.

Wrapping Up Chapter One

Unhealed childhood trauma lingers into our adult lives and becomes our default mechanism of existence without our conscious realization. When we become aware of our wounded inner child and tune into our triggers and blindspots, we realize that the issues we have as an adult have their roots hidden and buried in the unresolved traumas of our childhood. As adults, we hold the responsibility to connect with the little one inside of us and pour infinite amounts of love into them so they know we're on their side again.

In the next chapter, we will be talking about trauma in the brain and the effects of toxic stress on a child.

CHAPTER TWO: TRAUMA IN THE BRAIN

"The wound is not my fault, but the healing is my responsibility."

Marianne Williamson

Childhood trauma leads to adults living in survival mode, too afraid to plant roots, plan for the future, trust others, and let joy in. It's a blessing to go from surviving to thriving, but it takes acknowledgment of what has happened and the willpower to heal ourselves. What happened to you in your childhood is unfortunately beyond your control and definitely not your fault, yet the severity of the effects of childhood trauma in adulthood are real. It's so easy to start blaming yourself for the trauma you experienced, but you need to give yourself the gift of your own tenderness and compassion. Even now, as broken as you may feel, you are still so strong. There is something to be said for how you hold yourself together and keep on moving, even though you feel like shattering. Stop being so hard on yourself, this is your healing, and it doesn't need to be pretty or magical; you just have to keep going.

The trauma you experienced as a child had tangible effects on your brain and impacts your life to this day. Although this chapter may be a bit technical, it's important to understand what happened to know why you feel and think the things you do. Understanding the effects of trauma on your brain is so important because you will be able to better understand yourself and how to help your inner child heal.

The Three Types of Stress

We have all experienced some sort of childhood stress. It could have been your first day at a new school or the fight between you and your best friend. However, a little bit of stress from time to time is healthy; it helps us develop problem-solving skills and facilitates our growth. The problem comes in when the stress is ongoing, and the responders in our bodies are always triggered. This causes long-lasting effects on the young brain that can carry into our adult lives. Stress contributes to a significant part of the development of a child. There are three types of stress: positive stress, tolerable stress, and toxic stress, and they all have an impact on the brain.

1. Positive stress

Positive stress is short-lived and is characterized by an increased heart rate and elevation of stress hormones. It is normal and actually an essential part of healthy development. Positive stress is triggered during minor stress experiences like starting a new job, meeting new people, moving homes, receiving an injection, or even something like a rollercoaster ride. When children experience positive stress in a supportive environment, it helps them gradually learn how to deal with adversity and solve problems that develop a healthy stress response system.

2. Tolerable stress

Tolerable stress activates our body's alert systems to a greater degree and can be more serious. Tolerable stress can be caused by severe, longer-lasting difficulties like the passing of a loved one, a car accident, or a natural disaster. When a child experiences tolerable stress, there is potential for damage to the brain if there is no one to nurture and protect them. If the child has encouraging and loving relationships, their brain and other organs will recover over time from what otherwise might be permanently damaging effects.

3. Toxic stress

Toxic stress occurs when the body's stress response is triggered too many times. Toxic stress occurs when there is strong, frequent, or prolonged adversity like abuse, chronic neglect, exposure to violence, caregiver mental illness or substance abuse, and the accumulated burdens of family economic hardship. This kind of prolonged stress physically affects the brain and can disrupt the development of a child's brain architecture and other organ systems, leaving certain parts of the brain rewired. Toxic stress also increases the risk of cognitive impairment and stress-related diseases well into adulthood. The worse the childhood trauma, the greater the effects when we're grown up.

How Toxic Childhood Stress Affects the Brain

When the brain is continually exposed to a traumatic situation, it will shut down to protect itself from that environment. The brain will continue to function, but its growth rate drastically slows down. This creates vulnerability to depression and anxiety, and less resilience to stress. Toxic stress can affect us at any stage of life. The long-term effects differ depending on age and stage of brain development when we are exposed to the stress. The younger our brain, the more damaging the effects of toxic stress are. When the brain is young, it develops, grows, and absorbs so much of what it is exposed to in the environment, making it incredibly vulnerable to chemical influences like stress hormones that can cause long-term changes.

Toxic stress causes long-lasting or even permanent damage to the brain. The amygdala, prefrontal cortex, and anterior cingulate cortex are all affected. The amygdala is the fear center and detects anything dangerous in our environment, but it can become overstimulated due to toxic stress. When the amygdala is damaged by toxic stress, it is always telling our body that we are in danger, which results in chronic stress, where we feel permanently anxious, fearful, and irritated. Toxic stress causes the amygdala to significantly increase in size, and the affected child can develop symptoms similar to post-traumatic stress disorder. Victims will also often overreact to minor stress triggers because the amygdala has been sensitized, which means lower levels of stress now trigger the fear response.

The prefrontal cortex is responsible for our rational thinking and regulates our stress response system by making things appear less scary than they are. The prefrontal cortex controls our memory, emotions, and sensory processing in day-to-day life. This allows us to effectively use our bodies in certain situations, like when problem-solving. However, toxic stress causes the prefrontal cortex to decrease in size and impairs the functioning of the brain regions responsible for memory, learning, and executive functioning. As a result, the child may suffer from difficulties with concentration, attention, and absorbing information. When the body is under stress, it releases cortisol from the adrenal glands. Cortisol is the hormone responsible for our fight-or-flight reaction and increases blood pressure, heart rate, muscle tension, and respiration. If the cortisol levels are too high in the body, it affects a child's ability to think clearly or reasonably. The result of toxic stress is that the body always thinks it's in danger, so there are constant high levels of cortisol in the body, affecting the child's ability to focus and learn.

The anterior cingulate cortex is another region of the brain negatively affected by toxic stress. This is the emotional center of our brain and controls and manages unpleasant emotions during stressful situations. If the anterior cingulate cortex is damaged by toxic stress, the child will have trouble regulating their emotions. For example, if someone plays a seemingly harmless prank on the child, they could remain frightened for long after the joke ends.

4 Ways Childhood Trauma Changes a Child's Brain and Body

Trauma in our early childhood can result in cognitive delays, disrupted attachment, and impaired emotional regulation, to name a few. The overdevelopment of certain pathways in the brain and the underdevelopment of others can lead to impairment later in life. Here are four ways that childhood trauma changes a child's brain and body:

1. Hormonal level changes

As mentioned earlier, cortisol is the stress hormone that prepares our body to take action or run away when faced with danger. Cortisol directs blood flow to major muscle groups in the body to activate survival mode and causes the thinking part of the brain to take a back seat. High levels of stress hormones cause an elevation of blood pressure which weakens the heart and circulatory system. It also leads to elevated glucose levels, resulting in type 2 diabetes. The other negative effects of abnormally high glucose levels are a compromised immune and inflammatory response system which can cause osteoporosis, lupus, multiple sclerosis, abdominal obesity, and depression. If a child's hormone levels are disrupted during the rapid brain development stages, it can have a drastic impact on the functioning of the brain and other organs, resulting in lifelong mental and physical health issues.

2. Immune system changes

The immune system is comprised of multiple cells, tissues, and organs and protects the body from allergies, infections, and inflammatory responses. Trauma and toxic stress are linked to thymus involution, which is the degeneration of the lymph nodes and spleen, telomere shortening, and increased stress hormones, which weakens immunity and increases inflammation. An impaired immune system and higher inflammation in the body increase the risk of diabetes, cardiovascular disease, cancer, viral infections, autoimmune diseases, asthma, allergies, anxiety, and depression.

3. Neurological changes

When we are born, the brain has around 100 billion neurons, which are almost all the brain nerves we will ever have over our lifetime. The connection between the brain neurons develops our hearing, vision, language, and higher cognitive functioning. Toxic stress and childhood trauma reduce the neural connections between the brain nerves in the prefrontal cortex, the thinking region of the brain. This region is dedicated to rational thinking, learning, and reasoning, and therefore trauma has a negative impact on cognitive ability. Incessant stress and trauma can weaken the remaining neural pathways in the prefrontal cortex and strengthen the pathways in the survival part of the brain. This causes the brain's rational region to function in the background while the survival part takes charge, making some children less capable of coping with adversity as they grow older.

4. Epigenetic changes

Epigenetics is the study of how our environment and behaviors can cause changes that affect the way our genes turn on and off, known as gene modification. For example, you may be born with the genetics to be confident and tall, but if you are abused and malnourished as a child, you are likely to have stunted growth and be a fearful adult. Trauma can provoke epigenetic changes for genes related to obesity, addiction, mental well-being, immune function, metabolic disease, and heart disease. Long-term epigenetic changes occur in the brains of adults with a history of childhood trauma.

How Does This Translate into Adulthood?

Childhood trauma can result in many psychological issues, and some adults even suffer from PTSD, although they may not even be fully aware of it. Adults who suffer from childhood trauma and toxic stress experience significant consequences on an emotional, physical and mental level. Emotionally, adults often experience feelings of worry, shame, guilt, helplessness, anxiety, depression, hopelessness, grief, and anger. Physically, adults who were exposed to trauma and abuse may develop a condition called *heightened stress response.* This impacts the ability to regulate emotions, leads to sleep difficulties, lowers immune functioning, and increases the risk of physical illness and disease throughout adulthood. Mentally, adults with a history of childhood trauma have heightened anxiety, depression, addictive tendencies, thoughts of suicide and self-harm, and relationship difficulties.

You might be thinking to yourself, "Well, there's no hope for me." But the relieving news is that's why we're here. All of these problems, no matter how "long-lasting or permanent," can be solved. The first step is recognizing that they are, in fact, problems in your life, and the next step is a whole lot of care, love, and patience. One of the most effective ways to overcome trauma is time, and you've already taken a step toward putting in the effort needed to heal yourself. Recovering can be a lengthy and trying journey, but with enough persistence, support, love, and of course, inner child healing, you can finally be free of that burden. In the wise words of Mahatma Gandhi:

"Strength does not come from physical capacity; it comes from an indomitable will."

Wrapping Up Chapter Two

This chapter is not meant to scare you or make you feel like all is lost. It is intended to show you how severe childhood trauma can be on your mind and body and that it should not be taken lightly. Your trauma is not your fault, but it is up to you to take a step towards healing. If your childhood wounds are not closed and healed, the damage will still affect you today as an adult. Now that you are aware of the effects of toxic stress and the damage that childhood trauma causes mentally, physically, and emotionally, we can move onto healing your inner child.

In the next chapter, we will talk about empowered healing, having an open mind and heart, and cultivating a mindset that will help you on your journey.

CHAPTER THREE:
EMPOWERED HEALING

"Trauma robs the victim of a sense of power and control over their own life; therefore, the guiding principle of recovery is to restore power and control to the survivor. They must be the author and arbiter of their own recovery."

Adapted from Dr. Judith Herman

Although it may not always feel like it, you are the author of your own story, and you can begin writing a new chapter any time you choose. You are the only one who can heal yourself, and you must make the conscious decision to do exactly that. The healing journey is about processing your past experiences, the ones your inner child still clings to. It's about sitting with the uncomfortable feelings, shifting your mindset to one of positivity and healing, and working through the trauma so that you can emerge a new, revised version of yourself.

You Need to Want to Heal

Healing oneself takes time, effort, thought, and energy. It requires purpose and determination. But most importantly, it requires the *want* to heal. Healing cannot happen unless you consciously make the decision to heal and work towards it. Trust me, I know. You want it all to disappear, the pain, the nightmares, the anxiety, the flashbacks, and the feeling of hopelessness that consumes you. You want to be free of the constant weight dragging you down. You want it all to stop. But you *need* to *want* to help yourself. You need to want to heal for true change to occur. While other people in your life can provide support, guidance, and encouragement, only you alone can take the steps and actions needed towards healing your inner child.

The healing process is not linear. It doesn't happen instantaneously; instead, it manifests itself in small yet delightful doses of "normal." Healing is hard work, but it's necessary work. Nobody wants to feel pain or relive their traumatic experiences, but you can't heal unless you feel it. Emotional pain cannot kill you, but constantly running from it can. You need to allow the feeling to surface and embrace it to find true, cellular-deep healing. It's going to hurt, but every moment you're feeling something, you're doing the work. Every moment you feel that ache in your gut, you're healing. The only way out is through. When you allow yourself to sit with the discomfort and accept that you are doing work, you can silence your internal critic that believes that feeling pain means you're "doing something wrong." Instead, you begin to understand that feeling your pain is important and productive. When you understand the true nature of your work, you can summon compassion for yourself as you move through your uncomfortable feelings on the path to peace, healing, and wholeness. It took me a long time to figure this out and silence the ego in my head, but now this framework has changed my life.

When doing the inner work necessary to heal, you need to treat yourself like a cherished friend. Be sympathetic and attentive, and treat yourself with kindness. Trust the process, no matter how difficult it may be. Sometimes you might feel like you're over a certain trauma, but the wound reopens. Don't give up or get discouraged. Just take it one day at a time and show yourself some *grace*.

The G.R.A.C.E. Method

Compassion can change your life. Remember that you have been criticizing yourself for years, and it hasn't brought about anything positive. It's time to start accepting yourself and see what happens. The GRACE approach is five steps you can use to help you heal and cultivate some compassion towards yourself and your inner child.

G – Give yourself permission to grieve

Experiencing trauma always involves some form of loss. It may not always be a tangible loss, but it can be a loss of well-being, naivety, normalcy, or life. You need to give yourself the time, space, and permission to deal with the losses you've accumulated throughout your life. Let yourself feel the emotions, they're valid, and your trauma matters. Grief is like the ocean; it comes in waves, ebbing and flowing. Sometimes the water will be calm, and sometimes it will be overwhelming. Allow the grief to come freely and fully because doing so allows the healing to occur.

R - Reward your altered self

Trauma generally wreaks havoc in our lives, and it takes time to put the pieces back together. There is a good chance that the ideals, beliefs, and values you once held dear to you are distorted or even shattered, and you're left with a void. You need to work on rebuilding yourself with what's left as well as your new insights. It might feel touch and go at times, and you may often feel doubtful that the new you will hold itself together. But eventually, you will learn to trust yourself enough, and as you work on this new you, you need to pause, congratulate, and reward yourself. You didn't ask for any of this, but you're here and putting in the work, which is something to be proud of. Acknowledge your progress and reward yourself with some much-needed self-care. Go for a massage, take a holiday, watch your favorite movie during the middle of the day, buy a keepsake to commemorate your perseverance, take a bath, make a cup of tea or spend the afternoon reading. You deserve to be loved and cared for, especially by yourself. Don't you dare let that little voice in your head tell you otherwise.

A – Accept where you are along your healing journey

You need to destroy the idea that healing has timelines and deadlines. Accept wherever you are in your healing journey and be patient with your progress. It's okay if you spend months journaling and feel like you're over the trauma, only to have it hit you all again. It's okay to join a support group, attend it regularly and then have a complete breakdown even though you thought you had it under control. It's okay to dive into heaps of books, only to feel like none of the words make sense and stop reading altogether. You are not weak. Healing is messy. It's a process, and there is no timeline, especially when it comes to grief and pain. Tell your voice of self-criticism to sit down and be quiet. Accept where you are with an attitude of compassion, wherever that may be.

C – Connect with others. Connect with yourself

When we're emotionally wounded, we have a tendency to retreat into ourselves, and we pull back from society and all emotional connections. Trauma sends us to a deep, scary place, and we often fall into a volatile state – emotionally, physically, relationally, and spiritually. Trauma is a dark force that pulls us into a devastating state of mind. Connection is the tool that helps bring us back. As you move through the healing journey, you need to find yourself again. You need to rediscover who you are through conversation (that could look like therapy or counseling), meditation, reflection, prayer, and relationships. By finding a connection to yourself and others, you can work towards understanding the pain, integrating the loss, and creating cohesion in the chaos. You may find that you have pushed people away (and rightly so sometimes), but the good news is that the worthy ones will come back, and you can work on repairing your relationships. You'll also make new connections with people who are like-minded. True recovery requires both reconnecting with yourself and others.

E – Encourage yourself to continue the healing

Sometimes it can seem easier just to wander through life, dulling the ache inside with distractions, than to do the necessary work and find healing. And some people may choose that route (no judgment here), but I promise you that things are a lot better on the other side. Healing also means more than just surviving. It's about overcoming the trauma, not just building a life around the pain. If you choose to find true healing, it's important to encourage yourself. So what does this encouragement look like? It's acknowledging the effort it takes just to get up in the morning. It's recognizing your progress, your achievements, and your obstacles. It's affirming your desire to heal, every single day. It's talking to yourself reassuringly like you would talk to a good friend. It's sharing your healing journey in whatever way you feel comfortable doing. It's also a lot of introspection – you're alive, you've survived, and you've grown. Encourage yourself, care for yourself and support yourself through your healing journey. You deserve nothing less.

Keep an Open Mind

When it comes to healing, it's normal to feel uncertain about the idea of your inner child. If the whole concept makes you hesitant, you can look at this "inner child" as a depiction of your past experiences. It is merely a way of exploring your relationship with the past. For most of us, our past is comprised of a combination of positive and negative events. These circumstances are the building blocks of our character and guide our ambitions and decisions as we grow older and reach adulthood. Having a deeper understanding of the early experiences that shaped us in our past can be the key to enjoying life now as an adult. The process of connecting with the inner child can be beneficial for every single person who has experienced childhood trauma, and anyone is capable of doing it. But often, the lack of belief that you can make that connection presents a barrier. However, the key to inner child healing is *acknowledging* your inner child. It is a process of self-discovery.

The Importance of Mindset During Healing

One of the most essential and often missing pieces to true healing is your mindset. Your mind is powerful, and cultivating a healing mindset does take work. However, this mindset is essential to your healing journey if you want to see the best results.

What is a mindset?

A mindset is the set of beliefs, attitudes, and values that determine how we view ourselves and the world around us. Our mindset influences how we think, act, and perceive the situations we come across. A mindset is a set of assumptions, methods, and ideas that shape how we experience life. Do you feel like your life is in your control, or are you destined for a specific path? Do you feel like life happens to you or for you? Do you believe in growth, or are you content in your comfortable way of living? There are two predominant mindsets; a growth mindset and a fixed mindset.

Someone with a fixed mindset believes that certain traits like intelligence or talent are fixed, set at birth. A person with a fixed mindset lets success or failure define them. They spend a lot of time documenting their talents and less time developing them and believe that talent alone creates success. When faced with failure or a challenge, people with a fixed mindset will tell themselves and others that they can't do it or will make excuses to rationalize the failure. You've probably heard of someone being stuck in their ways. This is a typical example of someone with a fixed mindset.

On the other hand, a growth mindset is built on a person's belief that their most basic abilities and talents can be developed through hard work and dedication. Their successes or failures do not confine them. People with a growth mindset believe that they can be so much more. Their mindset is based on the notion that brains and talent are just a starting point.

The fortunate thing about mindset is that it can be shifted. You can change how you view yourself and the world, your ideals and beliefs, perceptions, and assumptions. Along your healing journey, having a growth mindset is crucial. You need to believe that you can change and that you can heal. As Tony Robbins says:

"If you do what you've always done, you will get what you've always gotten."

The Power of Mindset When Healing

Our thoughts are actually energy, and our brain activity can be measured without physically touching the body. Every single cell in our body responds to energy. The genetic expression of our cells literally turns on or turns off in response to the energy of our thoughts. When we think negative thoughts, it sends a message to our cells that things are not good. When we think positive thoughts, a healing response is stimulated. That is how powerful our thoughts are when it comes to healing. Admittedly, it's not always easy to feel positive when you're miserable, but creating a positive healing mindset will make you feel better.

Our brain's ability to change with repetition, known as neuroplasticity, allows it to change and adapt over time. Neuroscience studies have shown that repetitive behaviors grow our brain matter, regardless of our age. This also refers to positive thinking. The more consistent our positive thoughts are, the more our brain neurons change their chemical signals, which alter the structure and functioning of the brain associated with positive behavioral changes and healing. The changes in our brain can be positive or negative, depending on the consistency of our behavior, for example, meditating daily or drug addiction. The brain changes can go either way. The late Henry Ford said it perfectly, "Whether you think you can or think you can't, you're right." Our mindset affects everything, and maintaining an open and positive mindset is so important for healing.

The Placebo Effect

Neurobiological research[i] over the past thirty years has indicated that the placebo effect can lead to healing outcomes. The placebo effect stems from a person's mindset or anticipation to heal. It triggers specific brain areas connected to pain and anxiety that activate the physiological effects that result in healing.

A person's mindset can also lead to a nocebo effect, which is negative. For example, during the study, patients were told that an injection would hurt, and they automatically had a heightened pain response. Other patients were informed about the potential unwanted side effects of a medication, and they had an increased presence of those effects.

The research from the study also suggests that mindset influences the benefits that people get from certain behaviors. For example, a person's mindset around how caloric or indulgent their food was impacted the physical effects of the food. Another study demonstrated that viewing stress as positive and helpful instead of negative and harmful was associated with increased emotional and physical well-being and more productivity at work.

Our mindset can be a very effective tool when given the chance. By controlling our thoughts and shifting our mindset toward the positive, we have the ability to change our outcomes, and that is some powerful stuff!

5 ways you can change your mindset

Here are the tools I've used over the years to create a healing mindset that has brought me to where I am today – healed, happy, healthy, and thriving!

1. Challenge your limiting beliefs

Nearly all of us hold onto limiting beliefs that inhibit us from achieving our aspirations and goals. Once you are able to challenge and overcome these beliefs, the world is your oyster. However, if we let our limiting beliefs overpower us, we will continue to live in a negative rut. Our limiting beliefs are the stories we spin about who we think we are, fat, stupid, shy, undeserving of love or success. They aren't true, but they become our truth if we accept them. We can replace our limiting beliefs with empowering ones, and that way, we will reach our full potential.

2. Face your fears

Our fears are real, and we cannot ignore them and expect them to disappear. Once you become aware of the fears entangled in your mindset, your whole perception will shift. That's not to say that they will go away, but a large part of their power gets taken away when we recognize the fear. Acknowledge your fears but don't dwell on them. Don't allow fear to preoccupy your thinking. What you focus on expands, so focusing on fear will only make it worse. You need to face the fear and focus beyond it. Try to see what is on the other side of your fear and focus on that.

3. Shift your perspective

Learning to shift your mindset from a place of negativity to one of positivity can seem overwhelming, but it doesn't need to be. Sometimes, the tiniest shift in how you view the world is all it takes to completely change your mindset forever. Shifting your perspective allows you to shift out of your usual point of view to discover new ways of thinking and understanding. One way to do this is to look at the meaning we assign to our experiences. Nothing in life has meaning except for the meaning you give it. Do you see the speed bumps in your life as challenges or opportunities?

4. Change your self-talk

Have you taken note of what the voice inside your head is saying about you? Is it saying positive, uplifting things? Or are your thoughts about yourself generally negative? Changing your self-talk begins the moment you wake up in the morning. It is all about shifting the narrative and planting positive language in your head when you start your day. It can be as simple as walking into the kitchen, seeing the dirty dinner dishes, and instead of being annoyed, thinking, "I'm so grateful that I have dishes to wash because it means I had food to eat." You might find that a positive mantra you can say repeatedly works for you. Or maybe you need to put together a list of positive affirmations that you can look at throughout the day. It's okay if you need to correct your course after negativity pops into your head; just remember that it's important to keep the positivity flowing. Surround yourself with an environment that reflects the mindset you want to have and bounce back from any setbacks by reminding yourself why you're doing this.

5. Get support

There is nothing wrong with seeking support if you're unsure of where to start. Working with a professional can be one of the most effective ways to shift your mindset because they've probably been in your shoes and know the best strategies to help you on your path to success. Getting the support you need will kickstart your healing mindset journey so that you can reap the most benefits.

Wrapping Up Chapter Three

Empowered healing is all about being ready to heal and making the decision to heal on your own. Once you've taken that step, you need to work on getting your mindset right. It's not going to happen overnight, but as long as you're working towards a healing mindset a little more every day, you're on the right path. Consciousness is where change happens, there are no quick fixes for healing, and the process is different for everyone. There are no timeframes. Be compassionate and accepting towards yourself and know that every small movement in the right direction is progress, and it all adds up.

The next chapter dives into healing your inner child and why it's so important. We will touch on some ways to start reconnecting with and healing the little one inside of you.

CHAPTER FOUR: INNER CHILD HEALING

"Inside every angry child is an emotion they haven't been able to comprehend and inside every angry adult is that child."

Unknown

We were all once children, and that child did not just up and vanish, to be replaced by a perfectly capable and always responsible adult. Your inner child still dwells within, yelling for attention, and until you recognize them and begin inner child work, you will keep experiencing outbursts of pain and anger that you cannot explain. Inner child healing is so important for so many people because it empowers you and helps you connect with your higher self to work on healing your wounded child with the powers of mindfulness, insight, and compassion. All you need to do is become aware of these healing powers and start practicing and applying them to your inner child to lead a joyful and rewarding life.

What is Inner Child Healing?

One of the biggest parts of inner child healing is the idea that we all have a younger self within us with different needs and experiences. Our subconscious minds remember everything, even if we don't. As we grow up into bigger bodies with more conscious and logical brains, our inner child doesn't just disappear. When we are triggered by situations in life and can't understand why, it's because the inner child inside of us is still very much present and crying for our attention. Our wounded inner child only wants care, love, and assurance, but as adults, we have a bad habit of ignoring these cries for attention, and we deny, dismiss, or block out our feelings. We look for a solution to fix ourselves, to bury the pain and pretend like nothing is wrong. These are all trauma responses that we experience in our adult life, and we respond to our wounds in the same way we learned as kids, utilizing the methods that helped keep us safe back then.

The fact that most of us don't even know about our inner child and can't actually see them is a sort of ignorance. Our inner children are wounded and need us to acknowledge them, but we choose to ignore them instead. This ignorance is ingrained in every cell of our body and consciousness, and it acts like a pair of rose-tinted glasses. Except the glasses we're wearing aren't actually rose-tinted, they're dark and gloomy and full of scratches. They stop us from seeing our reality, and we find ourselves doing irrational things that cause us more suffering. Just like ignorance is in every one of our cells, so is the wounded child. There is no need to look into the past for that child; they are always with us, their suffering is happening right now in the present moment, and we only need to look deeply within to reconnect with them.

Just like our anguish is present in every cell of our body, so are the seeds of awakening, understanding, and happiness. We just have to use them to help ourselves. When we become aware of the wounded inner child within, we cultivate an attitude of compassion for them, and we begin to generate an energy of mindfulness. We all have a part of ourselves that was never quite loved or supported in the way we needed as a child, and that's where inner child healing is so important. It is a way for us to address the needs that weren't fulfilled as children and heal the attached wounds that developed. Inner child healing is about creating a safe space where the subconscious mind can take the lead. Inner child healing is the act of going inward to explore our raw feelings and the parts of us that may have been rejected or labeled as *too much* by other people. Through introspection, we are able to begin peeling back our go-to coping mechanisms (the unhealthy ones like running away, burying, and numbing our feelings). We are able to accept our true authentic selves and integrate our subconscious into consciousness. We are able to make peace with our broken pieces.

Inner child healing helps you look back on your early wounds without judgment. As adults, we often look at our previous trauma through our adult perspective instead of seeing the experience through the eyes of a child. We tend to judge and invalidate the pain we may have felt. It may not have been a "big deal" in the long run, but the pain you felt at that moment was honest and legitimate and impacted your life. Learning how to reconnect with your inner child and validate their pain without judgment will help you better understand your own emotions and needs in the present moment.

Inner child healing is a way for you to learn to love and accept your inner child as a separate person. It is a way for you to tell your inner child that you recognize them and that your intention is to do everything you can to heal their wounds. It's about creating a safe, non-judgmental environment so that you can reconnect with your innocence. It is only by loving and healing your inner child that you can begin to love yourself again. Inner child healing is a way to empower yourself and focus on being mindful and present. The goal of inner child work is to heal your wounds and get back in touch with yourself prior to the harmful experiences or trauma. It is about reconnecting with the innocent joy and excitement you felt as a child.

Why Is Inner Child Healing Important?

On a psychological level, a wounded inner child could be the underlying cause behind low self-esteem, depression, anger, self-sabotage, abandonment issues, or relationship difficulties. Working with the inner child is the key to healing our past traumas and living a wonderful, fulfilled life now in the present moment. But beyond our emotional needs, inner child work is also important for other reasons. Here are a few points on why inner child healing is so crucial:

- It increases your self-awareness.

- You are able to uncover and heal any bottled-up emotions you experienced growing up.

- You can access any repressed memories that are holding you back and work through them.

- It boosts your self-esteem and encourages self-compassion.

- You learn to incorporate self-care into your day-to-day life.

- You gain personal power and the ability to set healthy boundaries.

- It helps you identify the root causes behind your fears or unhelpful patterns.

- It enables you to connect the trauma with certain behaviors in order to change your behaviors.

- You heal on a deep cellular level.

- You are able to tap into your fun, creative and playful side.

The best thing about children is that they don't care if they look silly. They dance, paint, cuddle stuffed animals, and drink their milkshake, reveling in the happiness those moments bring them. It is only as we get older that we begin to care what people think, and a huge part of that is because we've suppressed our child-like character. We don't acknowledge the inner child within us, so they never get a chance to come out and play, to explore, or experience the awe of everything around them. Inner child healing is so important because it encourages us to return to this child-like wonder. Taking a moment to pause and stare at the stars, to marvel at the lights at a theme park, or stand barefoot in the grass with nothing more important to do is what inspires us and nurtures our creativity. When we are unhindered by social expectations or regulations, we are able to dream and create again. Turning our trauma into curiosity and joy and having a childish young heart does so much for us as individuals and our relationships with those around us.

How to Start Healing Your Inner Child

The first step to start healing your inner child has been mentioned multiple times already, but I am going to reiterate it because it's just that important. You need to acknowledge your inner child, even though it might feel silly. Giving your inner child an identity can help you work through the trauma you faced together. The acknowledgment process also involves recognizing and accepting that things caused you pain in your childhood. Bringing these hurts out into the light is important when it comes to understanding their impact. There are many ways to start communicating with your inner child, which we will discuss further along in the book, but the goal is to give your inner child the feelings of acceptance and validation that were absent for so long.

The next step is beginning to foster a wise inner parent. You need to accept whatever your inner child is feeling and embrace the emotion with tenderness and compassion. Many of us have an internal critical voice, and we are constantly telling ourselves what we should and shouldn't feel, and we shame ourselves for what we do feel. But as an adult trying to cultivate a wise inner parent, you need to make space for the emotions you're feeling and break the habit of shaming. Learn to accept and just be with what is there. Humans are complicated creatures, but it is important to observe, honor, and then practice accepting yourself and your feelings.

Blaming Your Parents

You may feel like your parents did a good job raising you with what they were given, or you may feel like they're to blame for everything. However, healing the inner child is not about unearthing everything your parents did "wrong" or getting angry at them. One reality that we all share as humans is that most of us have had one or more of our needs not met in childhood. In most cases, this is not of ill-intent of your parents. Very often, your needs weren't met because you were raised by caregivers who didn't know how to meet their own needs, so they could only model what they were capable of. An unhealed inner child is a form of generational trauma that can be passed on from parent to child. Your parents or caregiver could have been suffering from a wounded inner child and therefore passed on their pain to you. Sometimes overcoming generational curses means becoming your own parent. It is so important to take this step towards healing because when you heal yourself, you heal the next generation that follows. Pain will continually pass through the family line until someone is ready to feel it, heal it, and let it go.

It's okay to feel angry at the parents your inner child was raised by, but these emotions need to be processed and not buried. With this process comes the recognition that you are no longer that child and that you are no longer without your own personal power. Often after allowing ourselves to feel anger and sadness towards our parents, we find new understanding and compassion. We are able to see that no one is perfect, and they had their own struggles to deal with. It took me some time to realize that my parents were workaholics because that was their coping mechanism. They had deep-seated pain of their own, and working all the time was the only way they knew how to deal with it. I know they meant me no harm, and I came to realize that the responsibility to pull my life together was mine alone and became mine the moment I was old enough to take the wheel of my own life. The tough reality is that sometimes we're dealt certain cards in life, and it may not be fair, but it is our responsibility to choose to change our lives. It is easy to play the blame game, but holding onto anger only ends up hurting us. In some cases, it may feel impossible to forgive your caregivers or an adult that hurt you, but it is important to move beyond the blame and reclaim your wholeness. It is the only way to heal.

Wrapping Up Chapter Four

When you begin inner child work, you start to create the safety and security your younger self has always needed. Many people had to grow up too quickly and experienced constant fear and the need to protect themselves, but through inner child healing, you get to reconnect to that little one again. You can work through your pain and trauma so that you can see the world through the eyes of your healed inner child – eyes that sparkle in awe and amazement as they see magic, love, and mystery in the most ordinary things. Inner child healing gives your younger self the room to shine again, without the pain and the suffering from the past.

In the next chapter, we will expand on cultivating that wise parent through reparenting. We will cover the four pillars of reparenting and how this form of healing can help you nurture your inner child's needs.

CHAPTER FIVE: REPARENTING

"Although we may have suffered misfortune as a child, it is never too late to relive our childhoods and reconnect to that childlike side of ourselves. When we take responsibility for our happiness in life, we have the power to feel safe, heal ourselves, and create greater wholeness. This gift can never be taken away from us."

Aletheia Luna

Even if you can happily report that you enjoyed a wonderful childhood, it is safe to assume that there's stuff – great stuff and not-so-great stuff – that transpired in your younger years that impact the way you see the world, how you show up in your daily life and how you feel about who you are. In an ideal world, our parents are two self-actualized individuals who allow their children to be seen and heard as the unique human beings that they are. Unfortunately, the reality is that we live in a culture where we are not taught about conscious awareness, and as a result, most of us are born to unconscious parents. Unconscious parents repeat the same habits and patterns they grew up learning. They operate from a wounded place because of their own unprocessed emotions. Unconscious parents can only parent from their own level of awareness.

The fortunate truth is that no matter how deep-seated our beliefs and understandings are, we don't have to carry them around as emotional baggage forever. The idea of becoming your own parent may seem a bit out there at first, but through reparenting as a form of therapy, it is possible to learn how to parent yourself and heal your inner child.

What is Reparenting?

Simply put, reparenting is the act of giving ourselves what we didn't receive as a child. It is the procedure for revising and reforming the parent-ego state, which contains the behaviors and attitudes of the caregiver that are observed and copied by the child. As adults, we are unable to return to our childhood to begin again, so we need to reparent as a way to give ourselves what was missing from our first years of life. Originally, reparenting referred to a type of psychotherapy where a therapist assumed the role of a parental figure to treat psychological trauma caused by abusive or neglective parenting. However, in the case of the alternative forms of self-healing in this book, the term reparenting will be used in reference to techniques that you can personally use to reparent your inner child. A therapist can impart the knowledge on how to do this effectively; however, the ultimate responsibility lies with you.

No one but you can do the work, and you need to show up each and every day to take care of your shifting needs. It is your responsibility to teach yourself the tools you need to heal, and reparenting is one of those tools. Reparenting involves learning to give your wounded inner child the respect, care, dignity, and love they deserved when you were a little one. With reparenting, you can learn how to validate your feelings by observing them rather than instinctually criticizing or disregarding them. Reparenting cultivates an acceptance of yourself while honoring the needs of your inner child. Reparenting allows you to become the priority.

The Purpose of Reparenting

Reparenting arises from the belief that most psychological issues develop because children grow up without having their needs fulfilled. When children feel insecure or unloved, they often grow up into adults who have a tough time navigating relationships and coping with the challenges of life. Childhood is a crucial time when we learn the key fundamentals of life. If we don't learn them during the critical stages of our development, we either develop stunted fundamentals, or we end up not learning them at all.

According to experts, there are specific ages where we tend to develop certain emotional and psychological aspects of ourselves:

- Infant (age 0-3 years): trust

- Toddler (age 3-5 years): initiative

- Early childhood (age 5-11 years): self-esteem

- Adolescents (age 12-18 years): identity

If trauma is experienced as a child, it impacts our emotional development. Through reparenting, we can learn to take care of the vulnerable parts of ourselves, the parts that we dare not show the world. In essence, reparenting helps to give ourselves the encouragement, support, and love we've always craved. Reparenting can create a safe space for you to:

- Feel supported

- Be vulnerable

- Learn to trust

- Learn about your hidden underlying needs and how to meet them

- Be confrontational without fear of abandonment

- Finally experience a secure, healthy attachment

One technique you can use to find out if you need to reparent is to ask yourself the following three questions.

1. What are five words to describe your mother as you perceived her when growing up?

2. What are five words to describe your father as you perceived him when growing up?

3. Was there another significant parent figure? If so, what five words would you use to describe them as you perceived them when growing up?

If the words you choose are positive, you may not need to reparent. However, if the words you choose are all negative, it is an indication that reparenting is necessary. Most people tend to have a mix of positive and negative adjectives. These can be separated so that the positives can be consciously used and the negatives can be worked on through the reparenting process.

The Four Pillars of Reparenting

Reparenting is your own personal responsibility, and anyone can begin the process of reparenting themselves. It is not a quick fix, and it takes time, effort, commitment, and patience. It will require you to show up for yourself every day, but will help you to forgive and heal your inner child. You will develop a wise inner parent through reparenting, and you will learn how to trust yourself, maybe even for the first time in your life.

You can build this trust by setting small promises for yourself to fulfill daily through acts of self-care. You also need to start speaking kindly to yourself, as if you were talking to a child in pain. Start each day by asking yourself, *"What do I need? What can I do for myself today?"*

The more you do this, the more you will reconnect with your inner child and learn to hear what they have to say. It will become an automatic response to the world around you that will help reconnect you to your intuition.

These are the four pillars to reparenting:

1. Emotional Regulation

Emotional regulation is the skill to successfully navigate your emotional states. Parents co-regulate with their children a lot. They soothe and support, which allows the child to internalize the process, and in time, they are able to do it for themselves. As a result, when the child is distressed or hurt, they know how to regulate themselves. As adults, emotional regulation is our way of coping with stress in a flexible, tolerant and adaptive manner. When we regulate our emotions, we create a homeostatic baseline that allows us to respond responsibly when triggered and safely navigate the highs and lows that we face during life. Many of us need to develop our ability to regulate ourselves emotionally. We need to have go-to methods of looking after ourselves by staying calm. The methods will be specific to you and what works in your life, but common practices include deep belly breathing and breathwork, meditation, and relaxation techniques like tai chi, yoga, and qigong. When triggered and in distress, we need to immediately regulate through breathing, boundaries, and containment. However, other emotional regulation through daily practice will help us maintain a deactivated nervous system that is not so quick to get triggered. And if it is, it can return to normal quite swiftly.

2. Loving Discipline

For many people, discipline has a negative connotation, and our inner child likes to rebel against the whole idea of it. However, discipline is a significant part of the healing journey, and cultivating it supports us in showing up for ourselves. It needs to be emphasized that this act of discipline is a loving one. Teaching ourselves discipline as grown-ups is one of the best gifts we can give ourselves. We can do this by implementing small but meaningful, healthy behaviors, boundaries, and rituals that are maintained over time, resulting in a positive effect on our lives. Discipline can be cultivated by making and keeping small promises to ourselves and developing daily routines and habits. In the context of inner child healing and reparenting, we seek to create the guidance and healthy boundaries that may have been lacking when we were little. This process should be approached slowly. Notice uncomfortable or painful moments throughout your day and ask yourself, *"How do I want to care for myself right now? If I was a child, how would I parent myself at this moment and show myself guidance and love?"*

This in itself is discipline; you're beginning to create a lifelong practice of caring for yourself. The discipline does not need to consist of boundaries that are too rigid. It is developing confidence over time so that if you take a day to rest, you are confident the ritual or habit will still be there to return to. A great example of creating a form of loving discipline is establishing a morning routine to start your day off that includes positive activities like meditating, using mala beads, affirmations and journaling.

3. Self-Care

This pillar goes hand in hand with loving discipline, and in many ways, reparenting and self-care are the same thing. Recently the term self-care has gotten a bad rap and is used to justify self-indulgence. However, true self-care is supporting your needs and acknowledging your worth. It is not self-indulgent but rather fundamental to the healing journey. Self-care is all about truly looking after yourself as you go about life. It is the act of learning to recognize and look after your physical and emotional needs and wants, especially those denied in childhood. Often self-care is considered to be a hot bubble bath or spending the day watching your favorite movies, and while those are lovely and important, self-care is deeper than that. The most important aspects of self-care are compassion, exercise, nutrition, and sleep. In this modern and manic world we live in, it is not uncommon for us to forget that our bodies need care and support to run effectively. And if we're not taking care of our bodies, we can forget about taking care of our minds. Self-care is all about having a *back to basics* attitude because meeting our needs with consistency and commitment will regulate us emotionally and stabilize our moods so that we can confidently face life.

During my own healing journey, I came to realize that self-care is about having boundaries with draining people or situations, doing weekly shopping for wholesome food, getting enough quality sleep, asking for help when needed, doing more of what I love and managing my workload to prioritize time to exercise and do what I want to do. Once these basics are met consistently, we can begin adding beautiful, mindful, feel-good practices to feed our souls.

4. Joy

The fourth pillar is one of the ultimate goals of doing the reparenting work. One of the best parts about reparenting is allowing ourselves to rediscover our childlike sense of wonder. This wonder is made up of a combination of imagination, creativity, spontaneity, and playfulness, and it is fundamental to who we are. Nurturing and creating space for childlike wonder in our adult lives is so important. Most people have forgotten how to experience true joy, and we don't often prioritize it because it doesn't pay the bills, or we have completely reclassified what it means. Joy is simply playing for the sake of playing; it is having passions, pursuits, and interests independent of our responsibilities.

When it comes to finding true joy, you'll likely need to fight parts of yourself that tell you that you're selfish when wanting to do things just for the joy of it. Chasing joy is good for our mental health; it staves off depression, increases happiness, and reminds us that life is a gift and not a chore. We need to learn to do things for our enjoyment and not for any external reward. So, arrange a fun activity, eat your favorite meal from when you were little, listen to your favorite fail-safe-feel-good album, or call a friend and laugh wildly. Just like a wonderful, enthusiastic parent would arrange something that brings the greatest joy to their child, it's time for you to do the same thing for yourself and your inner child – every day!

Depending on your unique childhood experiences, some of these pillars will be more challenging than others. For me, loving discipline was the hardest part. I was often too tough on myself, and my inner child rebelled. It was a journey of grieving for my past self and finding compassion that allowed me to view discipline in a new light. Reparenting can be quite challenging, and you need to have patience with yourself. However, when you relearn who you are and how to connect to your inner child, it will truly change you for the better. The process of reparenting will bring you so much empathy, compassion, and creative energy.

Here are five steps that I have found helpful to begin this process:

1. Breathe

It is so easy to become overwhelmed, especially when faced with the four pillars of reparenting. This healing does not happen overnight or even over a couple of weeks. It takes a lot of consistent effort, and sometimes you need to take breaks, or you'll become exhausted and fall back into old patterns. Be as dedicated to the pillars as you can, and remember to breathe through the uncomfortable feelings. In chapter nine, we will be covering breathwork and how to breathe for inner child healing.

2. Keep one little promise to yourself every day

This promise should be so small that it is seemingly insignificant. You need to choose something that puts you in a position to succeed. For example, the first promise to myself was to go to bed earlier. I knew that with my schedule, I could do this every single day. But if you have a schedule that won't allow for this, it's not a good choice for you. If you aren't exercising consistently now, don't promise yourself that you'll go to the gym every day; that is not setting yourself up for success. Some good, realistic examples are to meditate for two minutes daily, go for a five-minute walk around the block in the evening, cook one healthy meal at home every day, or journal before bed every night. Time is important here, so don't choose a promise that takes more than ten minutes in total.

3. **Tell someone you trust that you're beginning the process (except for your parents)**

You do not need to share what you're doing with your parents; it is not necessary and may be hurtful to them. Remember that they did the best they could with their level of awareness and will probably become defensive if you talk about it with them – it's human instinct. The reparenting process is for you and not them. If you have a close friend or a caring partner, let them know that you're taking this step towards your healing. The support will be helpful.

4. **Use this mantra every day**

"What can I give myself right now?" This is a mantra that I still use often. As children, we don't always receive what we need, so as adults, we have the opportunity to give what we need to ourselves. When strong emotions surface, ask yourself this question. Sometimes the answer might be a bubble bath, and other times it might be to disconnect from social media or get into the sun for a few minutes. It's also okay if you ask yourself this question and there is no answer.

Just continue asking. It's all about practicing to connect with your intuition, and if you stay committed, you will get the answers.

5. Celebrate yourself when you show up

If you were not recognized, seen, and celebrated for the unique individual that you are, you will be quick to disregard the fact that you are showing up now. Reparenting is difficult – it's soul work – so acknowledge the courage it takes and own your progress. Start celebrating the person you're becoming and the victories along the way, no matter how small.

Wrapping Up Chapter Five

The beliefs and patterns we develop as a child stay within, controlling our lives until we question them. During these early stages of childhood, we learn to validate our feelings and process our emotions, but if we are not given these psychological tools, things can get messy later on. That is why it's so vital to develop our sense of self-awareness through reparenting. Otherwise, we will never become conscious of why we behave the way we behave or are the way we are.

Instead, we will perpetuate the never-ending cycle of trauma and emotional immaturity through our wounded inner child. It is time to break the cycle, and reparenting is a powerful tool to do that with. It is important to foster a wise parent, develop a secure attachment with yourself, validate your inner child, and create an intimate relationship with them. Reparenting is all about providing your inner child with safety, consistency, encouragement, and nurturing care.

It is important to remember that reparenting is a process and a practice that takes patience and heaps of compassion. You are about to become the parent (to yourself) that you always wanted, so be gentle and be kind.

In the next chapter, we will talk about the energy of mindfulness and why it is important for inner child healing.

CHAPTER SIX: THE ENERGY OF MINDFULNESS

"Wherever you are. Be all there."

Jim Elliot

Mindfulness is the basic human ability to be fully present, with awareness of our thoughts, emotions, bodily sensations, and environment. It is about being in the moment of where we are, what we're doing, and seeing what's going on around us through a gentle, nurturing lens. Being mindful involves acceptance. It is about paying attention to our thoughts and feelings without judgment – without believing that there is a *right or wrong* way to think or feel at any given moment. When we practice mindfulness, our thoughts tune into what we are sensing in the present moment rather than revisiting the past or thinking about the future.

Mindfulness is a quality that every one of us already possesses. It does not need to be conjured up; you just have to learn how to access it.

What is The Energy of Mindfulness?

The energy of mindfulness is what heals our inner child. It is the energy that helps us to be entirely present. When we are completely present, with our mind and body truly together, we become fully alive. So how do we cultivate this energy?

To understand our minds, we need to understand our consciousness. The consciousness can be divided into mind consciousness and store consciousness.

Mind consciousness is also known as the *conscious mind* and is our active awareness. It is the working part of our consciousness that plans, judges, worries, analyzes, and uses up most of our energy. Mind consciousness consumes twenty percent of the body's power. So simply put, using mind consciousness is very taxing; worrying, judging, and planning use a lot of energy.

Being mindful keeps us in the present moment and allows the mind consciousness to relax and let go of the energy of predicting the future or worrying about the past. We can save our energy by training the mind consciousness to form a habit of mindfulness.

The second layer of consciousness is *store consciousness,* also known as root consciousness because it is the base and the deepest form of the conscious mind. Store consciousness is where all our past experiences are stored. It is the unconscious mind that has the capacity to process and learn. The first aspect of store consciousness is a place of storage where all kinds of seeds of information are kept. The second aspect is that store consciousness does not just take in all the information; it also holds it and preserves it. The third aspect of store consciousness is the sense of processing and transforming. Our minds are often not with our bodies, figuratively speaking, of course. Sometimes we go through our day-to-day activities without the first layer of consciousness, the mind consciousness, being active at all. We can perform many tasks from store consciousness alone, and our mind consciousness can be wondering about hundreds of other things.

For example, have you ever driven home after work and you have little recollection of the journey once you arrive home? You know you were in the car and driving, but you don't remember much else. That is because the mind consciousness is not even thinking about driving. But thanks to the store consciousness operating on its own, you were able to reach your destination without having an accident or getting lost. The effort of processing on this level is not costly. Store consciousness does not spend as much energy as the mind consciousness does. Store consciousness can manage information without a lot of work on your part.

You can compare consciousness to a house. The living room is the mind consciousness, and the basement is the store consciousness. Our emotions like happiness, sadness, and anger reside in the store consciousness in the form of seeds. We have seeds for many different feelings like a seed for mindfulness, compassion, and empathy, a seed for fear, despair, and judgment, a seed of understanding and kindness, and so on. Our store consciousness includes the entirety of the seeds and the soil that protects and supports them. The seeds remain there until we use our five senses to awaken a seed that makes us feel a feeling like happiness, sadness, or rage. The seed comes up from the basement of store consciousness to the living room of mind consciousness. It is now no longer a seed but a mental formation. The term formation refers to something that is created by various circumstances coming together. A flower, your hand, and a house are all formations. The house is a physical formation. Your hand is a physiological formation, and the seed that has manifested is a mental formation. When someone awakens the seed of sadness by saying or doing something that hurts us, that seed will come up and manifest in the mind consciousness as a mental formation. Sadness is just one example of this. In the store consciousness, sadness is a seed, and in the mind consciousness, sadness becomes a mental formation.

Whenever a seed, for example, the seed of fear, comes to the living room and manifests as a mental formation, the first thing we need to do is awaken the seed of mindfulness and invite it to join as well. Now there are two mental formations in the living room, which become the mindfulness of fear. Mindfulness always refers to mindfulness of something; when we sit mindfully, that is mindfulness of sitting. When we do yoga mindfully, that is mindfulness of yoga. When we eat mindfully, that is mindfulness of eating. So in this example, the mindfulness is mindfulness of fear. The mindfulness recognizes and embraces the fear. The practice of mindfulness is based on the comprehension of nonduality – fear is not an enemy. Both aspects of mindfulness and fear are ourselves. The mindfulness is not there to stifle or battle against the fear but rather to acknowledge it and take care of it, just like a big brother would help a younger brother. The energy of fear is recognized and accepted gently by the energy of mindfulness.

Whenever we need the energy of mindfulness, we just need to awaken that seed through mindful walking, breathing, or smiling. The energy will come up to the living room, ready to do the work of recognizing, embracing, looking intensely, and transforming. To cultivate the energy of mindfulness, we need to try and engage our active awareness in whatever we do. We want to be mindful as we sip our tea or walk through the park. When we drive, we want to be aware that we are driving. When we do breathwork, we want to be aware that we are breathing. No matter what we do, we want to practice nurturing the energy of mindfulness so it becomes effective. Within the seed of mindfulness is a seed of concentration, and with these two energies, we can free ourselves from the afflictions we face.

Mindfulness and The Inner Child

Mindfulness is one of the ways through to our inner child. We need to embrace them exactly where they are – caught by the past, scared, and enraged at being abandoned for so long. We need to awaken the seeds of our childhood suffering from a grown-up state of awareness and mindfulness. This will make it safe for our inner child to come out from under the bed. We need to have the courage to bring healing to our hurting inner child and transform ourselves. Once we awaken the seeds of mindful healing in ourselves, the energy of mindfulness extends into everything we connect with on a quantum level. Through mindfulness, we can take our inner child with us into our daily life. Through mindfulness, we can bring healing and transformation to the ingrained patterns passed onto us from our ancestors – behaviors built up over time that intensifies the fears and pain of the wounded inner child.

The Function of Mindfulness

Here are three important functions of mindful inner child healing:

1. Recognize your inner child

The first function of mindfulness is to recognize and not put up barriers. You need to stop and become aware of the little one within you. When you recognize your wounded inner child for the first time, all you need to do is be conscious of them and say hello. Perhaps your inner child is sad. If you notice this, just breathe and say to yourself, "As I breathe in, I know that sadness has manifested in me. Hello, my sadness. As I breathe out, I will take good care of you."

2. Embrace your inner child

Once you have acknowledged your inner child, the second function of mindfulness is to embrace them. This is a very pleasant part of the practice. Instead of battling your emotions, you are choosing to embrace them tenderly. The first few minutes of recognizing and embracing your inner child with compassion will bring some much-needed relief. The difficult emotions will still be there, but you won't suffer as much anymore.

3. Comfort and relieve your inner child

After acknowledging and welcoming your inner child, the third function of mindfulness is to calm and relieve your difficult emotions. And this is done by gently holding your inner child. You will begin to soothe the painful feelings and can begin to feel some peace. When you embrace your strong emotions with mindfulness and concentration, you will be able to see the roots of these mental formations. You will know the origin of your suffering, and your pain will lessen.

Mindfulness recognizes, embraces, and relieves. If you have mindfulness, and you know how to keep the mindfulness awakened, concentration will be there too. If you know how to keep the concentration awakened, insight will follow. The energy of mindfulness will enable you to look deeply and gain the awareness you need so that transformation is possible.

How to practice mindfulness

At the core, mindfulness is a practice that needs to be repeated regularly and with intention. We need to build mindful routines in our daily lives to bring ourselves back to what matters. When we practice mindfulness, we are practicing the art of creating a space for ourselves and for our inner child. A space to think and breathe, a space between ourselves and our reactions.

Here are some things to know before practicing mindfulness

- There is no need to buy anything fancy. Mindfulness can be practiced anywhere, at any time, and you don't need a special cushion or mat. All you need is to devote some time and space to expand your awareness skills daily.

- The goal is not to quiet your mind. Unless you're a Buddhist monk who has been practicing for twenty years, there is no way to completely silence your mind. Too often, the goal of mindfulness is made out to be complete mind stillness, but in actuality, it is to pay attention to the present moment without judgment.

- Your mind will wander, and that is okay. As you practice mindfulness and pay attention to what's happening in your body and mind in the present moment, you might find that niggly thoughts arise. A wandering mind isn't something to fear; it is part of human nature. In fact, when your mind wanders, it is a magical moment for an essential piece of the mindfulness practice. Researchers believe that the moment you recognize that your mind has wandered and consciously bring it back to the present moment can lead to a healthier, more agile brain.

- The judgy part of your brain will try to take the wheel. We are all guilty of listening to our inner critic, but an important part of the mindfulness practice is to be without judgment. That's not to say the critical side of your brain won't try to take over; it just means that we need to practice investigating the judgments and diffusing them. By doing this, we can choose how we perceive and react to things. When practicing mindfulness, try not to judge yourself for any thoughts that arise. Simply make a mental note of them, let them pass, recognize any sensations they leave in your body, and let those pass as well.

- Mindfulness is all about returning your attention to the present moment. It may feel like the mind is wired to get carried away in thought, which is why mindfulness is the practice of returning to the breath over and over again. The sensation of our breath is the anchor to the present moment, and each time we consciously return to it, we reinforce our ability to do it again.

Putting Mindfulness Into Practice

Cultivating a habit of mindfulness is not always easy, but it's important to remember that mindfulness is a natural quality we all possess; it just takes a little bit of practice and commitment.

Here are five simple ways to incorporate mindfulness practice into your daily life:

1. Start your day with a mindful morning

Intention refers to the underlying motivation for everything you say, do, and think. When you act in unintended ways, there is a disconnect between the quicker, unconscious impulses of the lower brain center and the slower, conscious abilities of the higher brain centers like the pre-frontal cortex. Your unconscious brain is responsible for most of your behavior and decision-making. So, practicing mindfulness can help you align your conscious thinking with the emotional drive that the lower centers of your brain care about, including motivations like connection, purpose, reward, core values, and self-identity. By setting an intention, you are able to help strengthen the connection between the lower and higher centers of your brain. This will change your day, making your actions, words, and responses more mindful and compassionate. Setting an intention is best done first thing in the morning before checking your phone or email.

- Once your alarm has gone off, sit in your bed or a chair with a relaxed posture. Sit upright but not rigid. Close your eyes and connect with the sensations of your body.

- Take three deep, nourishing breaths, inhaling through your nose and exhaling through your mouth. Then let your breath fall into its own rhythm and simply become aware of it, noticing the rise and fall of your chest and belly as you breathe naturally.

- Ask yourself, "What is my intention for today?" You can use these prompts to help you with the answer. As you think about everything you will face today, ask yourself:

  ○ How can I show up today to have the greatest impact?

  ○ What quality of mind do I want to develop and strengthen?

  ○ What do I need to do to take better care of myself?

- How can I be more compassionate to myself and others through difficult moments?

- How can I feel more connected and fulfilled?

- Set your intention for the day ahead. For example, "Today, I will be kinder to myself, be more patient with others, give generously, persevere, stay grounded, eat well, and have fun," or anything else you feel is important and relevant.

- Check-in with yourself throughout the day. Pause, take a few deep breaths, and revisit your intentions. As you become more conscious of your intentions, the quality of your mood, communication, and relationships shift.

2. Eat your food mindfully

It's so easy to eat a plate of food without even noticing what you're doing. Yet, eating is one of the most pleasurable experiences we can engage in as human beings, and eating mindfully can turn eating into a richer experience. When you bring your attention to your body and what you are truly hungry for, you can nourish all of your cravings. Here are some steps to follow before you eat:

● Take a few deep breaths before eating. It's common to move from one task to another without even pausing or taking a breath. By pausing, you slow down and allow a more calm transition into your meal. Bring your attention inward by closing your eyes and breathing deeply in and out of your belly before you begin eating.

● Once you are done breathing, listen to your body and bring your awareness to the physical sensations in your belly. Ask yourself, "How hungry am I feeling?" Try to really listen to your body and not your thoughts.

● When you're more in touch with how hungry you are, you can eat according to your level of hunger. You can mindfully choose what, when and how much to eat.

- While you're eating, continue to breathe deeply. Your body can digest your food more easily when you are relaxed.

3. Rewire your brain by pausing

It is estimated that 95% of human behavior runs on autopilot or *fast brain*. Your default brain signals are so efficient that they often cause you to relapse into old behaviors before you remember what you're meant to be doing instead. Mindfulness is the exact opposite of this process – it slows your brain down. It enables you to have intentional decisions, willpower, and actions. Mindfulness is a practice, and the more you do it, the stronger the executive control (*slow brain*) part of your mind will get. Every time you do something new and deliberate, you stimulate neuroplasticity that activates your grey matter, which is full of new neurons that aren't groomed for "fast brain" yet. The problem with humans is that the slow brain knows what's best for you, but the fast brain causes you to shortcut through life. So how can you trigger yourself to be mindful when you need it most? This is where the concept of "behavior design" comes in. It is a way to put your "slow brain" in the driver's seat, and there are two ways of doing that. The first way is to slow down the fast brain by placing obstacles in its path and the second way is by removing obstacles in the slow brain's path so that it can gain control. Here are some ways to shift that balance:

- Literally put an obstacle in your way so that you trip over what you want to do. If you want to meditate or do yoga, put your mat or cushion in the middle of the floor so you can't miss it when you walk past.

- Refresh your triggers regularly. For example, if you choose to use sticky notes around the house to remind yourself of your new intentions, it might work for about a week. After a while, your fast brain starts looking over the notes, and the old habits take control again. Try writing new ones every week and sticking them in slightly different places so you keep noticing them.

- Create new patterns in your day-to-day routine. Try a series of *if-this-then-that* messages to create easy reminders for yourself to shift into slow brain. For example, "If kettle, then deep breath" as a way to shift into mindfulness when you're about to make a cup of tea. Or, "If office door, then deep breath" to remind yourself to be mindful before starting your workday. Each intentional action to shift into a place of mindfulness will strengthen your slow brain.

4. Activate your mind and your muscles

Exercise can be a great form of mindfulness practice. Whether you're lifting weights, riding a bike, doing yoga, or dancing, instead of simply working out, you can choose to breathe and move in a way that gets your blood pumping and shifts you from feeling distracted to *in the moment* and capable. Use these steps to synchronize your body, mind, and nervous system when working out:

- Have a clear aim for your workout or activity. As you tie your running shoes or put on your swimsuit, set an intention and bring purpose to the activity by envisioning how you want to guide the session. As you climb on your bike, you could say, "I will breathe purposely and notice the sensations of the breeze, the sun, and the passing scenery."

● Warm up with simple moves and concentrate on matching the rhythm of your breath to your movement. Moving rhythmically will result in your brain activity, heart rate, and nervous system stabilizing and aligning.

● When you pick up the intensity, continue coordinating your movement and breath. Challenge yourself with more repetitions, a heavier weight, or faster speed, and notice how alert and alive you feel.

● Once you're done, slow your pace and close your eyes. Notice all the feelings in your body, the heat, the tingling, the shakiness, whatever it may be. Quietly acknowledge the symphony of sensations flowing in and around you and try and name what you sense and feel.

5. Drive your car mindfully, not manically

Driving can be stressful, especially in heavy traffic surrounded by impatient drivers. The flight or fight response is often activated when you get behind the wheel, which is why road rage erupts, and stress levels are through the roof. But it doesn't have to be like that. The chaotic traffic jam can provide an excellent opportunity for you to build your mindfulness muscle, restore your balance and perspective and increase your sense of connection to others. Here are some steps to a straightforward behind-the-wheel practice that works wonders.

- Make sure you are breathing. You'd be surprised how often you forget to breathe properly in stressful situations. This simple yet profound advice will help bring more oxygen to your body and widen the space between the stimulus of traffic and your increased stress response. Within this space lies choice and perspective.

- Ask yourself what you need. At that moment, you might need to feel safe, relieved, and at ease. Understanding your needs will bring balance.

- Give yourself what you need. If relief is what you need, you can scan your body for any tension and soften the pressure or adjust your body as needed. You can add in some compassionate affirmations like, "I am at ease, I feel safe, and I am happy."

● Take a look around you and acknowledge that all the other drivers are just like you. They all want to feel safe, happy, and have a sense of ease. You'll probably notice several drivers who look frustrated, but you might also catch someone smiling or singing. This will dissipate some of your own stress immediately.

● Take some more deep breaths. You can completely turn your mood around by applying these simple steps. When you feel the frustration of traffic arising, choose what you need to work on, affirm positivity and pass that thought on to others.

A Mindfulness Body Scan Meditation

Chapter ten is dedicated to meditation healing. However, I am including this powerful body scan meditation for mindfulness here for you to practice.

Body scan meditation is a great way to release any physical tension you might be holding onto. By mentally scanning yourself, you bring yourself into the present moment and bring awareness to every single part of your body.

How to Do a Body Scan Meditation

As with all kinds of meditation, doing a body scan is intended to be simple. Here are some instructions to get you started:

1. Get comfortable by lying down, particularly if you're doing a body scan before bed. If lying down is not possible or comfortable, you can also sit up.

2. Take some deep breaths, breathing from your belly instead of your chest. Allow your abdomen to expand and contract with each breath.

3. Bring awareness to your feet, followed by your attention. Observe any sensations in your feet. If you notice discomfort or pain, acknowledge it

and any emotions or thoughts that accompany it, and gently breathe through it.

4. Breathe into the tension. Focus your attention on any sensations, breathe into them and see what happens. Visualize any tension leaving your feet through your breath and evaporating into the air. Move onto the next part of your body when you are ready.

5. Scan your entire body this way. Gradually move up from your feet until you reach the top of your head. Acknowledge and feel where you are holding stress, tightness, pain, or pressure and continue to breathe through the sensations. This will help you release tension in your body in the present moment and be more aware of it in the future so you can release it then as well.

Wrapping Up Chapter Six

It may take some time for you to digest this chapter; I know that mindfulness is not the easiest concept to wrap your head around. However, as you practice, remember to be compassionate and patient with yourself. You are working on rewiring your brain for the better, and that is no small task. Cultivating a habit of mindfulness will help you become more mindful of your inner child during the healing journey. It is crucial to be mindful of your inner child's wants, needs, and emotions. That way, you can support them and make progress with healing them

The next chapter will cover the importance of noticing and validating yourself and your inner child. It is important to give yourself the validation you have needed your whole life to set boundaries and work through any triggers that are causing your inner child any pain.

CHAPTER SEVEN: VALIDATE AND NOTICE YOURSELF

"Release old concepts and energies that keep you in self-punishment patterns. Release old stories and create from a place of love and self-validation."

Gautama Buddha

Part of the reparenting process is validating and noticing yourself as well as your inner child. From the time we are born, we need validation, but we often don't receive this in our childhoods. That's where self-validation comes in, especially when healing your inner child. Self-validation is a skill that takes practice, and at first, it won't be easy. If we received very little validation while growing up and never saw our parents validate themselves, we would have no idea how to validate ourselves. This was the case for me, but now I know that self-validation is not only possible but absolutely necessary to feel happy, secure, inwardly peaceful, worthy, and have loving relationships with others.

Validation and Reparenting

When we enter this world, we look for outward signs that we matter. As a child, it is a question of will the environment respond to my hunger? Will my parents respond to my cries? As little ones, we are constantly looking to our external world to gauge how responsive it will be to us and our needs. This validation helps us orient ourselves in the world. Through this, we develop the idea that we either matter or we don't, that we are safe or unsafe, or that the world is responsive to us or not.

Ideally, every parent should validate the needs of their child by showing them that they hear, see and understand their needs and wants. This is called *mirroring and echoing* and is especially important when a child is non-verbal. Mirroring involves showing the child that they are seen. It is noticing and attending to the cues they display, either through physical touch, facial expressions, or an action that is appropriately responsive to the child's cue. For example, if a baby displays a cue for hunger through crying or showing signs of irritability, the parent would provide the baby with food. As soon as the child shows that they're full, the parent would stop feeding. If a child displays a cue of tiredness, the parent should notice and ensure the child is in a safe environment to sleep. If a child is smiling or happy, the parent should respond back with a smiling face. Echoing is showing a child that they are heard. It involves talking with the child in an appropriate tone and timely manner. Echoing is about engaging with the child and letting them know their voice is heard and important (even if they aren't even able to form words yet).

Every child is different, and so their cues will be different. It is the parent's responsibility to understand their individual child so that they can validate them through mirror and echo. It is important to note that parents won't be able to validate their children all the time. Why? Because parents are still human beings, they need to be present for themselves and listen to their own needs and wants, which is okay. The problem comes in when the mirroring and echoing are neglected, and the child is not validated on a pretty consistent basis. This will result in the child not developing a sense of validation that their needs and wants matter. If a child's needs and wants are not validated, as they get older, they will become more and more unaware of their own inner signals that let them know what they truly need and want. They will be unable to read their own cues or won't understand how to notice them because they've been disconnected from that part of themselves for so long. If a child cannot discern their own cues, they cannot validate themselves by responding to their own needs and wants. Therefore, they end up looking to others to do this for them by seeking the parent they wish they'd had. As adults, it is our inner child that is seeking validation, and it is up to us (not anyone else) to provide that for them.

Important Lists to Create When Validating Yourself

Some important lists to create during the reparenting process of validating and noticing yourself are a list of your needs, a list of things that make you feel nurtured, and a list of boundaries.

The Power of a List

Lists are wonderful because they go beyond the tasks we need to accomplish or the things we need to buy. Lists are an easy and effective way to reconnect with how we feel about what's going on in our life. They help us understand what truly matters, determine where we'd like to go next, and remind ourselves of the good things.

Three Key Benefits of Lists

There are many benefits to making lists, but here are three key ones:

1. Lists clear your mind

When you put things down on paper, it is a way for you to clear your mind. Instead of trying to remember one hundred different things, you can simply look at your list.

2. Lists give you a birds-eye view

Creating a list can help you take a step back and gain some perspective. When you put everything that's going on in your mind down on paper, it's easier to see the bigger picture. Lists can help you feel less overwhelmed because you are able to clearly see everything that needs to be done.

3. Lists help you think on paper

The true power of a list is that it helps you think on paper. When you let thoughts bounce around in your head, it's easy for them to get distorted. However, it's easier to be more objective when things are down on paper. When you write things down in a list, you are able to refine and simplify your thoughts.

Reasons to Use Lists

Here are a few main reasons why it's helpful to use lists to help you in your healing journey:

- You can use a list to analyze your options and decisions, as well as your thoughts and feelings.

- Lists can help you identify your priorities.

- You can use lists to help you focus on one thing at a time.

- Lists can be used to help you deliberately forget things so that you can let them go from your mind.

- You can use lists to help you manage large amounts of information.

- Lists serve as great reminders of everything you need to remember to do.

- You can use lists to help you sort, rank, and prioritize things that will help focus your energy and attention.

A List for Your Needs

The first important list when it comes to your healing journey is to write down all of your needs. Having your needs written down is a helpful reminder to reference when you feel like your needs are not being met. This list will also be beneficial when defining and creating the boundaries needed to protect your inner child. These needs can be a combination of physical and emotional – they are whatever you feel you need to be happy and whole.

The first step to writing down a list of your needs is to tune into your body. Use the mindfulness practice from the previous chapter and do a quick body scan, noticing your mental and physical state. Identifying where you're at emotionally and physically is the first step in figuring out what you need. Once you've taken note of how you're feeling, jot down what you need in relation to those feelings. The idea here is to take all the thoughts floating around your head and turn them into solid, actionable needs.

A List of Comforting Phrases

The second list is one of comforting sayings. Make a list of things or phrases that make you feel nurtured. For example, a warm bath, a long walk in the afternoon, meditation, chocolate cookies, breathwork, a cozy bed, a rainbow, or hearing the words, "I am here for you, you are loved." These phrases are anything that can help you self-soothe and make you feel loved and validated. You can check in with this list when you feel emotionally triggered to nurture yourself as part of the reparenting process.

A List of Your Boundaries

The final list is one of the healthy boundaries you need to keep you happy and protect your inner child. Many of us have the wrong idea about boundaries, but establishing healthy boundaries is essential in your healing journey. Healthy boundaries are crucial for successful relationships with the people around you. Boundaries result from understanding your needs and using your voice to bring them to light. We all have a limit or a line we don't want to be crossed, but very often, those limits are violated by other people. In general, this is not malicious, but simply because people are not aware of our limits because we aren't clear with what we need. There are six boundaries that are essential to every human being. Here they are and an example of what they look like in practice.

1. Physical boundaries

These boundaries include your need for personal space, your acceptance of physical touch, and physical needs like needing to eat, sleep and hydrate. It is okay to implement your physical boundaries by letting people know you need space or you need to rest.

Some examples of healthy physical boundaries include:

- "I am a handshake person, not a big hugger."

- "Please respect my personal space and leave some distance when speaking to me."

- "I need to take a break; I am tired."

Physical boundary violations can vary from mild to severe, and some examples of these violations include:

- Being told to keep walking when you're tired, hungry, or thirsty

- Being touched inappropriately or being physically assaulted.

- Having someone enter your personal space without permission.

2. Emotional boundaries

These boundaries are about acknowledging and honoring your energy and emotions. It is important to know how much emotional energy you are capable of absorbing and setting boundaries accordingly. Emotional boundaries involve knowing when to share your feelings and when to not, especially for those who respond badly. Emotional boundaries also mean recognizing other people's feelings and respecting their ability to absorb emotional energy.

Some examples of healthy emotional boundaries include:

- "I don't really feel like talking about this now; it's not the right time."

- "When I open up to you and get criticized, it makes me shut down. I cannot share my feelings with you unless you are open to listening respectfully."

- "I'm having a difficult time right now and need to share. Are you able to listen?"

Some examples of emotional boundary violations include:

- Having your feelings dismissed or invalidated.

- Emotionally dumping on people without asking them first.

- Being told what and how to feel.

3. Time boundaries

Time is very valuable, and it is vital to protect how it is used. It is important to set time boundaries at work, at home, and in a social environment. To set time boundaries, you need to understand your priorities and set enough time aside for those priorities without overcommitting. Time boundaries help limit the amount of time you give to other people.

Some examples of healthy time boundaries include:

- "I can only stay until 5 p.m."

- "I would love to help, but I am not available today. Does tomorrow work for you?"

- "I can't make it to your party on Friday."

Some examples of violated time boundaries include:

- Asking a professional for advice or help without paying them.

- Being contacted during the times you said you were unavailable.

- Having someone demand that you help them or show up to an event.

4. Sexual boundaries

Healthy sexual boundaries include mutual respect, consent, privacy, and understanding of limits, preferences, and wishes.

Some examples of healthy sexual boundaries include:

- "That makes me uncomfortable."
- "I don't feel like having sex now."
- "Is this comfortable for you?"

Some examples of sexual boundary violations include:

- Not asking for consent.
- Criticizing a person's sexual preferences.
- Sulking or getting angry if a person does not want to have sex.

5. Intellectual boundaries

These boundaries refer to opinions, beliefs, ideas, and curiosity. Having healthy intellectual boundaries means mutual respect for a person's ideas and opinions. It is important to be respectful and willing to talk about an idea (from both parties) even if you don't completely agree. Intellectual boundaries also include considering whether or not it's an appropriate time to talk about something.

Some examples of healthy intellectual boundaries include:

- "I would love to discuss this more, but I don't think now is the right time."

- "I know that we disagree, but I will not allow you to belittle me like that."

- "I respect that we have different opinions on the matter."

Having intellectual boundaries does not mean you need to accept all beliefs and opinions. It is about recognizing the difference between healthy and unhealthy conversations and setting boundaries appropriately.

Some examples of intellectual boundary violations include:

- Having your valid opinion discredited or belittled.

- Letting someone know you do not tolerate the way they talk in the case of racism, sexism, homophobia, etc.

- Choosing to leave a conversation if it has no value to you.

6. Material boundaries

These boundaries include items of a material nature like your clothing, money, car, furniture, or house. It is important to have boundaries regarding what you can and cannot share with other people and how you expect your material items to be handled by those you do share them with.

Some examples of healthy material boundaries include:

- "I'm sorry, but I cannot lend you my bike. I use it every day."

- "We cannot let you borrow more money. We are happy to find another way to help."

- "Yes, you can borrow my jacket, but I do need it back by Monday."

Some examples of how material boundaries are violated include:

- Having something of yours stolen.

- Having your material possessions mishandled and destroyed when they are "borrowed" too often.

- Being manipulated and controlled through the use of money and possessions.

The Three Steps of Setting Boundaries

The reality of life is that we get what we tolerate, so unless we create clear boundaries, we will continue to get the things we allow. If we don't like something but keep tolerating it, we can't expect someone else to change without letting them know there is an issue. Until you make a clear request, other people aren't going to respect your boundaries. Here are the three steps to setting healthy boundaries.

1. Define your boundaries

Having strong boundaries means knowing what you enjoy, accept, and tolerate. It means knowing what the absolute deal breakers are for you in each area of your life. It means communicating your values, beliefs, desires, and limits to others. It means standing your ground when someone upsets you or crosses that boundary. It means protecting what you deem important. If you don't take yourself seriously, how can you expect anyone else to? The first step to setting healthy boundaries is to personally validate your own feelings and define what you need. Ask yourself, "What do I feel? What do I want? How can I make that happen?"

2. Communicate your boundaries

The next step is to actually tell people about your boundaries, which is a lot easier said than done, especially if it's enforcing a boundary that people are used to crossing. Many people worry that creating and instilling their boundaries will upset others and negatively affect their relationships. The reality is that, at first, this may be the case. If you are a person that rarely says no, then the first time you do so, the other person may be shocked and might rebel against your comments, hoping that you will back down and give in to their request. Therefore, you need to be clear and consistent with your boundaries and stand your ground. So, how do you do that? It is important to make sure your friend, family member, or colleague knows that you're establishing this boundary in order to have a better relationship with them moving forward. Clarity and compassion are key. Speak in a simple, clear, and gentle way that doesn't leave any room for a gray area. Use objective language; make it all about you, and don't point any fingers. Setting the boundary is about your well-being and not pointing out the flaws in other people.

3. Enforce your boundaries

Once you have set your boundaries with people, you may find yourself wanting to cave in or retract your comment. Instead, come up with a coping statement. When you're faced with the situation of wanting to back down, repeat the coping statement in your head. For example, "Setting boundaries is what I need and helpful for me to preserve my energy. What I need is important." Another example is, "Other people are entitled to their response, and I am entitled to be treated well and enforce my limits."

Once you have set your boundary, stand solid in what you've put out there. Giving in sends mixed messages, and it also teaches the other person that all they have to do to get their way is push harder, get angrier, shout a little louder, or argue with you a bit more. Remember, coping statements and self-soothing exercises are your friend for these times. When it comes to reinforcing your boundaries, repetition is key. Your habits become ingrained in your brain through repetition. Setting healthy boundaries is a habit you want to create, so you must keep practicing until the behavior becomes second nature.

Observing Your Emotions

Emotional observation promotes mindfulness, the ability to see the emotion for what it is without judging it or attempting to get rid of it. The beauty of observing your emotions is that once you do, you become in control of the feeling. I remember a specific point in my healing journey where I became aware of the power of observing my emotions. I was stuck in traffic on my way home from work, and another driver made me angry. I'll be honest, I can't even remember what they did, but at that moment, I felt furious and irritable. Then, while I sat in my car, I remembered something I had read about becoming a calmer and more mindful person. I had to observe myself and describe my emotions and what I was feeling in my body as if I were describing my medical symptoms to a doctor. I simply sat there and noticed what was going on inside me and ran through what was happening. I felt like a bit of a crazy person, but I described to myself how I felt enraged and how my stomach felt like it was in a knot. I described how my anger felt hot and enveloped my chest. And then the most amazingly bizarre thing happened; my anger completely vanished. I was dumbfounded. Usually, I was able to talk myself out of a negative state of mind some of the time by thinking about something else, but this was different. It happened so quickly and effortlessly.

That experience really struck me, so a week or two later, I tried something similar while I was meditating before bed one evening. That night, I felt sad and stressed out, and I had a feeling of heaviness over me. During my meditation, I kept pulling myself back into the present moment and simply observed and noticed how and where I was carrying those feelings. When I found them, I did not judge them or try to change them; I just observed them. Within a few moments, a strong feeling came over me, and the only way I could describe it was as a wave of *knowing* that told me, "These feelings are not you." It was such a soothing experience. I learned that I was an observer, and although my anxiety and sadness were a part of my real human experience, I saw them, and I realized that I didn't have to become engulfed by them or let them control my life.

What is Emotional Identification?

We cannot heal, change, or improve ourselves in any way if we don't have an awareness of what's going on with us. The following six points are a way for you to practice increasing your awareness. They are a way to practice observing and recognizing your feelings and sensations to discern what helps you stay in control emotionally and what sends your nervous system and emotion off the edge.

1. Create space for stillness

We as humans like to think we can multitask, but our brains actually can't. It might seem effortless to listen to a podcast while cooking or to check your notifications before getting out of bed, but we need to give our brains the opportunity to think and focus on one task. So go for a walk without music and leave your phone behind when you use the bathroom.

2. Notice your physical sensations

Being aware of the physical sensations in your body can be the first clue as to the emotions you're experiencing. You might find that anxiety feels like a tight ball below your sternum, or you get nauseous when you're stressed. It is important to locate the physical sensation of the emotion; it might stay there, it might move, or it might go away, but that's not important – simply being aware of it is.

3. Identify your emotion

Sometimes we aren't always aware of what certain emotions feel like or how to identify them. If you have a hard time identifying your emotions, you can make use of an emotion wheel. Start in the center and identify the core emotion, then work your way out.

4. Be curious, without judgment

We often judge what we should and shouldn't be feeling. When you notice these critical thoughts, try to move them from a place of judgment to a place of curiosity instead. For example, when you find your inner voice talking negatively to yourself, replace the thought with something like, "I notice that I am being critical of myself. I wonder what the real problem is. Maybe I am feeling nervous and overwhelmed."

5. Identify what you need

After you become aware of your physical sensations, recognize your feeling and notice what is happening within yourself, it is important to identify what you need. This will help you create an action plan to get your needs met.

6. Connect with the action

The above five points tend to happen in less than a minute, even though the process seems long.

Identifying your emotions really clicks the second you tune into the experience with curiosity and begin understanding your needs. Once you've identified the need, you can act on it and fulfill it.

Being able to connect our inner experience through our body's physical sensations, identifying our emotions, and responding effectively is one of the most powerful skills anyone can learn.

The following emotional acceptance exercise is one that changed my life, and I encourage you to practice it whenever you're having a strong emotion and are feeling overwhelmed by it.

1. Step one: identify the emotion

If you have more than one strong emotion, pick one to start with and go back to the others later if you need to. If you are having a hard time identifying the emotion, sit still for a minute and pay attention to your thoughts and the physical sensations in your body. Once you've identified your emotion, write it down on a piece of paper.

2. Step two: get some space

Now that you've recognized the emotion you're feeling, close your eyes and visualize yourself putting that emotion five feet in front of you. Sit like this for a few minutes, just imagining that you've put the emotion outside yourself so that you can observe it.

3. Step three: give your emotion a form

Now that you're visualizing the emotion out in front of you, ask yourself these questions and try to answer them.

- If your emotion had a size, how big or small would it be?

- If your emotion had a shape, what shape would it be?

- If your emotion had a color, what color would it be?

Once you've got the answers, visualize the emotion in front of you with the size, shape, and color you've given it. Observe it for a few moments, recognizing it for what it is. Once you're ready, you can let the emotion return to its original place inside of you.

4. Step four: reflect

Once you're done with this exercise, take a moment to reflect on what you've just experienced. Did you feel a change in the emotion when you put it out in front of you? Did the size, shape, and color make you feel differently about the emotion? Do you have changes in your reaction to the emotion? Does the emotion feel different now that the exercise is finished?

Wrapping Up Chapter Seven

Observing and validating your feelings are two very important parts of the healing journey. Observing your emotions and becoming aware of the need they're representing will help you identify how to meet that need. But a big part of observing your emotions is also recognizing that they are important and validating the way you feel. Your inner child has been ignored and invalidated for so long; it's time to make a change by noticing them, observing them, and embracing them.

In the next chapter, we will cover the power of self-love and self-care when it comes to healing your inner child.

CHAPTER EIGHT: PERSONAL HEALING – SELF LOVE AND SELF CARE

"When our inner child is not nurtured and nourished, our minds gradually close to new ideas, unprofitable commitments and the surprises of the spirit."

Brennan Manning

Personal healing is very important to the inner child healing journey. Not only do we need to focus on our inner child that was wounded all those years ago, but also our current adult self, who needs just as much love and care. First, we can start by making a list, as discussed in the previous chapter. Write down any physical or emotional neglections you notice for yourself, such as an unhealthy diet, poor hygiene, or emotional neglect from your partner. Having a list will help you focus on the areas that need change or improvement, making it easier to practice self-care for your specific needs.

Self-Care

Self-care is about maintaining a healthy and loving relationship with yourself. We often try and meet everyone else's needs and tend to forget about our own. Self-care is being conscious of our own needs, physically, emotionally, and mentally. Self-care is so essential for increasing our overall well-being and quality of life. The ultimate goal of self-care is to do whatever is good for our mind and body and satisfy our needs and desires. Through proper self-care, we can have better relationships with others because we are not pouring from an empty cup. Here are some wonderful ways to care for your body, mind, and relationships.

Self-Care Ideas for your Body

1. Oxygenate yourself by taking some deep breaths. Breathe into your abdomen, and let the air inflate your chest and stomach. We often forget to breathe deeply, and breathing properly is so powerful.

2. Make use of mindful movement by moving your body in a way that is different from exercising or working out. Mindful movement isn't about forcing yourself to do something because you have to. It is about tuning in to your body and asking yourself what you need. Find a way to get moving that makes both your mind and body feel good.

3. Finding a book (or many books) that resonate with you is an extremely important part of self-care and wellness. Lose yourself in a bookstore and then get even more lost in the books you choose to read.

4. Make small, healthy changes to your diet. Drink an extra glass of lemon water or have a detox day.

5. Make sure you're getting enough sleep, and if you're feeling tired, refuel your sleep tank and take a quick nap. All you need is twenty minutes!

6. Take a detoxing bath with some Epsom salts and your favorite essential oils.

7. Have a good laugh. Watch your favorite comedy or have a catch-up with a good friend.

Self-Care Ideas for the Mind

1. Meditation is a wonderful way to center yourself when life gets too stressful or your mind is racing at one hundred miles an hour. If you are unsure where to start or prefer guided meditation, I recommend downloading a meditation app. There are lots of useful ones out there!

2. Get some fresh air and go cloud-watching. Just relax on your back and mindfully watch the sky.

3. Do a mini-spring clean and donate any unused or unwanted items. Clearing your home is a great way to get good energy flowing again.

4. Keep a journal and write down your thoughts, feelings, daily happenings, or anything else you find interesting.

5. Get out of your comfort zone and do something that scares you, something you have never done before.

6. Scratch off a niggly task on your to-do list, something that you never get around to that's been there for ages.

7. Unplug from everything for an hour. Turn all your devices off and free yourself from the constant interruption of social media and email.

8. Take up a hobby that you really enjoy. You need to fulfill the creative, fun side of life as well.

Self-Care Ideas for Healthy Relationships

- No matter what kind of relationship you are in, make sure there is room for you. The most important relationship in life is the one with yourself.

- Vocalize your personal boundaries and say what you mean so there is no ambiguity. No one will know how you feel unless you speak out.

- Have realistic expectations. It is so easy to mismanage your own and other people's expectations in a relationship. So, be mindful of your role, the other person's role, and the limits of that position.

- Be open to new ideas and experiences. Change isn't always scary, and it may help you grow into a better you.

- Minimize people-pleasing out of guilt and only do something if that's what you really want to do.

- Understand that it's okay to say no sometimes, especially when you need to put yourself first.

- There are many reasons why people minimize the behavior of others, especially in close relationships. Whether it's a spouse, friend, or parent, occasionally check in with yourself about how you feel when you are with them. It has to start with you.

● Share your past with people who matter, whether it was wonderful or awful.

Connecting with Nature

Nature has the power to comfort, calm, and nurture our souls – nature *heals*, nature *soothes*, and nature *restores*. It is so important to reconnect with nature when it comes to your inner child healing journey. Here are some wonderful ways that nature can help you.

Nature Heals

Studies done in places like schools, workspaces, and hospitals have found that even a small piece of nature, like a plant in the room, has a significant positive influence on stress and anxiety levels. Being surrounded by nature, or even just looking at beautiful scenes of nature, increases happy and pleasant feelings and reduces negative feelings like irritation, anger, worry, fear, and tension. Being in nature not only improves emotional well-being but also enhances physical well-being. Research has shown that the positive effects of nature reduce the production of stress hormones and lower blood pressure, heart rate, and muscle tension. It has even been said that it can reduce mortality.

Nature soothes

Over and above the positive emotional and physical effects, nature helps us manage and deal with pain. Instinctively, every part of us is designed to find water, trees, plants, and other natural elements captivating. We are automatically drawn to scenes of nature and forget about any discomfort or pain when looking at them. This was reiterated through a study by a physician, Robert Ulrich, where he documented the results of patients who had gallbladder surgery. Half of the patients had a view of a wall, and the other half had a view of trees. The second half of the patients who had a view of nature tolerated pain better than those who didn't. Nurses reported that they had fewer negative effects and were discharged from the hospital sooner.

Nature restores

Another study done by Robert Ulrich and colleagues demonstrated that watching scenes of nature or spending time in nature directly correlates with a positive mood and psychological wellbeing, energy, and having a purpose. Spending time in nature has been shown to improve symptoms of depression, stress, and anxiety, leaving people feeling happier, calmer, and more balanced. Nature also increases our ability to concentrate. We instinctively find nature fascinating, and we can naturally focus on what we are feeling and experiencing in nature without getting distracted. Being in nature provides some rest for our busy minds and refreshes us for the rest of our day.

Self-Love

Self-love is accepting ourselves fully, treating ourselves with kindness and respect, and nurturing our growth and wellbeing. Self-love encompasses not only our thoughts and feelings about ourselves but also how we treat ourselves. So, when we conceptualize self-love, we imagine what we'd do for ourselves, how we'd talk to ourselves, and how we'd feel about ourselves – reflecting nothing but love and concern for who we are.

When you have self-love, you have an overall positive view of yourself. But this doesn't mean you'll feel positive about yourself all the time – that would be unrealistic, and it's okay! For example, I can temporarily feel upset or disappointed with myself but still love myself.

Self-Love Exercises

1. Create a ritual

For example, wake up fifteen minutes earlier to give yourself the chance to practice mindfulness and center yourself before the day ahead. You could take a lunchtime break where you mindfully take a five-minute walk around the block to get some fresh air. Another self-love ritual is going to bed earlier and taking the time to moisturize your skin. Be present in the moment and thank each part of your body for how strong it is and what it does for you. Spend some time in a moment of gratitude for yourself before bed each night.

2. Build a like-minded community

As much as we like to be independent, we cannot do everything ourselves. It is important to have love and care from like-minded people to help us stay motivated and feel supported. Positivity is contagious, and a strong community of people who care for you is something you'll need a lot of along your healing journey.

3. Make a "what's working for me" list

True self-love also means complete self-acceptance – the good, the bad, and everything in between. Creating a "what's working for me list" is one step you can take toward getting to a place of self-acceptance. This is a list of everything that helps you recognize what you already have going for you. Once you can see all the positive parts of your life down on paper, it will make it that much easier to love yourself.

4. Treat your body like a loving vessel

Be intentional and mindful about what you fuel your body with, not because you want to look great but because you want to feel great. Feeding your body wholesome, nutrient-rich food will boost your self-love and your energy.

5. Implement healthy boundaries

There is currently a culture of being a people-pleaser, and if you don't constantly say yes, you may be considered rude, bossy, and rigid. However, as we discussed in the previous chapter, boundaries are so important for your healing journey and your life as a whole. "No" is not a bad word, and it's not a bad thing to say it. Setting boundaries that protect your physical, emotional, and mental health will help you reclaim your personal power. Remember that you are only responsible for your reactions and no one else's, so if someone doesn't handle the implementation of your boundary well, it's not your fault or responsibility. That may sound harsh, but learning to say no and enforcing your limits is a sure way to build self-love.

6. The Emotional Freedom Technique (EFT)

The Emotional Freedom Technique, commonly referred to as "tapping," can reprogram your mind, body, and spirit for unconditional self-love. EFT works by using your fingertips to tap on acupressure meridians (the energy points used in traditional Chinese medicine) to release blockages. Focusing on the meridian points in the body restores the balance of energy by releasing the blockages caused by negative energy. When the body's energy flows naturally, there is a restoration of energy balance that relieves symptoms of negative experiences and the associated emotions. EFT works similarly to the needles used in acupuncture to restore the flow of energy. The tapping is then combined with acknowledging a specific issue, making strong positive statements concerning the issue, and creating reminder phrases or affirmations to facilitate emotional healing. EFT for self-love is a great way to heal any negative parts of your relationship with yourself.

Here is a general EFT tapping sequence:

- As you begin, you need to concentrate on the negative emotion – fear, anger or anxiety, a painful memory, an unresolved issue, or anything that's upsetting you.

● Before tapping, you need to find a setup phrase that describes the current problem or emotion you are faced with. The two primary goals you need to focus on are recognizing the issue (which can be done through observing your emotions) and accepting yourself despite your problems.

● A common example of a setup phrase is "Although I have this (emotion or problem), I deeply and completely accept myself." You can change the wording according to what resonates with you. However, refrain from addressing other people's issues as your own. For example, don't say, "Although my father is absent, I deeply and completely accept myself." Instead, you need to adjust the sentence by saying, "Although I'm feeling angry that my father is absent, I deeply and completely accept myself."

● While keeping your focus, use your fingertips to tap five to seven times on all nine of the body's meridian points (I recommend a quick internet search to learn more about these).

- Tap on these specific meridian points while focusing on accepting and resolving the negative emotion. Tapping will help repair any energy disruption.

- Tapping sends a signal directly to the stress centers of your mid-brain, which reduces the negative emotion or stress you get from your issue.

- Tapping will ultimately restore balance to your disrupted flow of energy.

7. Practice mindfulness

Our previous chapter on mindfulness is a wonderful practice to build up your self-love. Research has shown a link between mindfulness and elevated happiness and self-esteem, as well as lower levels of anxiety, which all make it easier to practice self-love. The love you have for yourself will be enhanced when you are aware of your thoughts, feelings, wants, and needs. By recognizing your needs (something you will become aware of during mindfulness practices) and taking action to meet them, you will boost your self-confidence and begin to prioritize your own self-interest rather than the demands and judgments of others.

8. Practice gratitude

Self-love and gratitude go hand-in-hand. Expressing your gratitude boosts self-esteem, which in turn will help you build or strengthen your self-love. When you take a moment to think about how much you have accomplished for yourself or others, you feel empowered. Often, people tend to focus on the negative experiences or failures in their lives, so learning how to be grateful for all the good things in your life can help reverse that frame of mind and put you on a path toward self-love and a more positive outlook on life.

9. Do something you're good at

Self-esteem and self-love are joined at the hip, and participating in a hobby or activity that brings you joy and that you're good at will not only boost your endorphins but will bring out the best, happiest version of yourself. If you love baking, then bake; if you enjoy dancing, then dance; if you love to run, grab those sneakers, head outside, and run.

10. Find your happy place

Think of a place that makes it easy just to be you. Sit quietly and embrace the present moment, not thinking about what's happening with work or what bills need to be paid. Just allow yourself to sit and be happy.

11. Build your letting-go muscle

We are always holding onto our past, which weighs heavy on our souls and can lower our self-esteem. So, the more blockages you clear from your life, the more you can really thrive in the area of self-love. Although getting rid of these blockages may be a way to protect yourself from hurting, it is also really only holding you back from moving forward and reaching optimal self-acceptance and loving who you are.

12. Affirmations

Affirmations are another way to increase your mood and promote self-love. They take your brain from a negative place to a positive place and reinforce new, healthy beliefs about yourself. Self-love affirmations can be used every day, and through repeated use, you will have more joy, confidence, bliss, and positivity. You will build your self-esteem, understand that you are worthy of love, release negative thoughts and feelings, welcome compassion and more consistent positive thoughts, and deepen your relationship with yourself and others. We will talk about the power of affirmations in the next section.

In the wise words of Buddha, "You, yourself, as much as anybody in the entire universe, deserve your love and affection."

Affirmations

Affirmations are short, positive, and powerful statements. They allow you to intentionally be in control of your thoughts. Affirmations are carefully constructed to have the most impact and can help you challenge and overcome self-sabotaging and negative thoughts. When you repeat them, they become the thoughts that shape your reality, and using affirmations can start to make positive changes in your life.

The formula for writing effective affirmations is important but easy to follow:

1. "I am..."

It is important to begin your affirmation with the words "I am," making it a lot more powerful. Using "I am" automatically gives your subconscious mind a command. Your mind then interprets it as an instruction that it must follow through on.

2. Use present tense

Formulate your affirmation as if you already have the thing or are the person you're talking about. Using present tense helps your mind visualize the outcome. For example, you can say, "I am healthy and fit," instead of saying, "This year I want to be healthy and fit."

3. Address what it is you want

Do not use any negatives in your affirmation because your subconscious mind does not recognize negatives (even if they are said in a positive light). If you say, "I won't shut myself off to new experiences," all your mind hears is *shut myself off*, which has a negative connotation. Instead, try stating, "I am open to new experiences."

4. Keep it short and sweet

There is no need to write an essay. It is much easier to remember something simple and snappy. For example, say, "I naturally choose healthy foods" rather than "I always choose healthy foods over junk food because I am mindful of my health."

5. Be precise

Include something very specific. This also makes it easier for your mind to visualize the result. So instead of saying, "I will increase my salary this year," say, "I am enjoying my $100,000 income this year".

6. Use strong adjectives

Another aspect of affirmations that makes it easier for your mind to visualize is using strong adjectives. Use words that evoke an emotion. For example, saying "I am an unstoppable force of nature" instead of "I can do anything." The one affirmation has a lot more feeling behind it than the other.

7. Make it meaningful

Make sure your affirmations mean something to you. They have to be meaningful on all levels and need to speak to all parts of you – your heart, soul, and mind.

How To Use Affirmations

Affirmations can be used whenever you want to make a positive change in your life. They are useful for when you're not in the best place – when you need a boost of self-esteem and support, when you're facing high levels of stress or demands at work, when your insecurity, grief, or heartache are taking control, or when you have setbacks in life. But that's not all. Affirmations are also very useful when you are in a good place, and you want to improve even more by developing good habits, becoming more mindful, increasing your productivity, and appreciating the people around you (to name a few).

To get the most out of affirmations, you will want to make it a regular practice and create a habit. Here is a general outline that you can follow, but it is also important to do what works best for you.

- Begin with 3 to 5 minutes of affirmations at least twice a day. For example, it is easy to do them when waking up and getting into bed. Perhaps you can make use of the time when you're putting on your makeup or shaving so that you can look at yourself as you repeat the affirmations. It is helpful to use an existing habit or action as a cue to make it much easier to form a new habit.

- Repeat each of your affirmations about ten times. Listen to yourself saying each word and work on believing it to be true. You might not believe it right away, and that's okay. *Breathe* into the affirmation while you're saying it. You want to move from a place where the affirmation is a concept to a real, positive embodiment of the quality you seek.

- Combine your affirmations with other positive thinking and goal-setting techniques. For example, affirmations work particularly well alongside visualization exercises, helping you give additional life and vividness to what you're saying. Combining your affirmations into a vision board is a great way to link the two practices together.

- Be patient. It will take some time before you notice any changes, so stick with your practice and trust the process.

Do Affirmations Really Work?

There is no magic when it comes to the effectiveness of affirmations – it is scientifically proven. The popularity and practice of affirmations are based on widely acknowledged and well-established psychological theories. The human brain has the ability to adapt and change when faced with different circumstances throughout life. Essentially, the way you use your brain will alter your brain. Both positive and negative thinking patterns create "train tracks" in your brain, and the more frequently a certain track is used, the deeper and more automatic it gets. You become what you practice, and that is how and why affirmations are so effective. Affirmations create positive tracks and alter the negative ones.

Affirmations have been shown to help with the tendency of holding onto negative experiences. When you are able to deal with negative messages and replace them with positive ones, you can construct a more flexible and optimistic narrative surrounding who you are and what you can accomplish. The idea behind affirmations is that it introduces a new and adaptive cognitive process which is very much the underlying principle of cognitive restructuring.

Another key psychological theory around positive affirmations is the self-affirmation theory which focuses on how people adapt to experiences or information threatening their self-concept. Some studies focus on the idea that your sense of self-integrity can be maintained by affirming what you believe in positive ways. According to the self-affirmation theory, the most important thing is that your affirmations reflect your core values and resonate with your sense of what is moral and worthwhile.

Surprisingly, your brain is not that good at deciphering the difference between imagination and reality, which can be useful. According to another study, creating a mental image of yourself doing something nerve-wracking, like conquering your fear of heights by skydiving, activates many of the same brain areas that would be activated if you were to actually experience the situation. So, regularly repeating affirmations about yourself encourages your brain to take these positive affirmations as fact. When you begin to believe you can do something, the actions will follow.

Affirmations in the Mirror

The mirror-gazing exercise is one of the most powerful inner child healing exercises you can do because it helps you communicate with your inner child in a powerful and direct way. This exercise allows you to talk to your inner child and give them the affirming words they wish they'd heard as a little one. The exercise is best done when you're feeling calm and not overwhelmed.

- Begin by standing in front of a mirror. Place your hand over your heart and look gently at yourself.

- Try and sense the presence of your inner child in your eyes. Observe your inner child from a place of inner guidance and consciousness.

- Practice giving your inner child a real and supportive presence. Your inner child wants to be seen and heard, so give that to them.

- Let your inner child know that you see them and you are ready to listen. Simply say, "I'm here."

- The first couple of times you show up for your inner child, they may react with intense emotion, disbelief, or distrust. That's okay – just observe those feelings without judgment.

- Once those emotions have settled a little, begin the conversation with something comforting and reassuring like, "I'm not going to abandon you again. I see you. You're so strong."

Here are some affirmations for your inner child that you can say in the mirror:

- *I deserve to be respected and treated with love.*

- *I acknowledge and accept that healing is possible.*

- *I do not blame myself for my childhood experiences and trauma.*

- *You are a divine being.*

- *You are safe.*

- *You are loved.*

- *You can trust yourself.*

- *You can do this.*

- *You deserve every bit of happiness and joy.*

- *It was not your fault.*

Another exercise for you to try is filling out the following blank affirmations. Remember to be true to yourself and your needs. Your affirmations are there to rewire any negative thinking habits you may have and boost your self-love.

I Am _____

You _____ and I love you

I promise to _____

I love you and will always _____

If you would like some more examples of positive, healing affirmations or to be guided through some affirmation exercises, I have an audiobook available on Audible called *Powerful Affirmations For Your Inner Child and Inner Child Healing: Self Affirmations.*

Gratitude

Sometimes being told to count your blessing and be grateful can be unhelpful and even somewhat offensive. I understand that sometimes life is really hard, and right now, things may look really bleak. But gratitude is not about diminishing how tough and unprecedented anything is or pretending that you are not anxious and that everything is fine. Gratitude is something that can exist alongside the very real and understandable trauma and negative emotions that most people experience when their inner child is wounded. Gratitude is not there to replace those emotions but rather to help you better weather and recover from this hurt and trauma. I know that it's hard to always feel grateful amid grief, anger, and stress, but I can promise you that gratitude does have healing powers.

During this time of healing, it is important that we not only focus on repairing our traumas and connecting with our wounded inner child but also be mindful of what we have now that keeps us going. Practicing gratitude is a great way to help us realize what we have to be grateful for each day while we are on this healing journey.

What is gratitude?

Gratitude is the expression of appreciation for what we have. With gratitude, people acknowledge the goodness in their lives. It is an acknowledgment of value independent of monetary worth. Gratitude helps us appreciate things on a deeper level. It helps us relish good experiences and feel more positive emotions. Gratitude is a spontaneous emotion, but, increasingly, research has established its value as a practice. Studies have shown that people can intentionally cultivate gratitude, and there are important social and personal benefits to doing so. Gratitude generates an attitude of positivity that both reaches inward and extends outward.

Ways to cultivate gratitude

Like I said earlier, gratitude is not meant to invalidate your trauma or hurt. But it is a way for you to shift your focus to concentrate on what you do have instead of what you lack. Although practicing gratitude may feel unnatural at first, a mental state of gratitude grows stronger with use and repetition.

Here are some ways to practice gratitude on a regular basis:

1. Meditate

Meditation and mindfulness practices involve focusing on the present moment without any judgment. Although people tend to focus on finding Zen or peace, it is also possible to focus on what you're grateful for in the present moment (the warm bed you're sitting on, the sun on your face, the cup of tea you're drinking, etc.)

2. Take notice

Become aware of your negativity, gossiping, or complaining. Take notice of how you see the world. If there is traffic, are you always angry and blaming the drivers around you? Do you allow your circumstances to dictate your mood, or are you able to breathe and shift into a state of calmness? Once you notice how you view things, you can begin to shift your thoughts to a place of gratitude. Try thinking, "I'm so grateful that I have a car, and it will get me where I need to go safely despite this traffic."

3. Keep a gratitude journal

Spend a few minutes each day writing down what you are grateful for. It doesn't have to be anything major – it could be as simple as being grateful for the socks on your feet. This will help you remember that there are still many things in life that you can be grateful for even when you are having a hard time. Feeling gratitude in any given moment, despite your circumstances, can shift your physiology and focus.

4. Switch your point of view

After you have started taking notice and writing, start switching your point of view from negative to positive, from upset to grateful. This will take time and practice but any time you catch yourself, just bring your mind back to the positive. You are responsible for your own thinking, and you can create an attitude of gratitude by simply saying that you feel that way.

5. Be humble

Humility is the "act of being respectful or modest." Think about what or who you take for granted and see if you can shift your position and attitude. Humility helps us to be open to new ways of thinking and experiencing the world.

6. Share your appreciation

Don't be shy to give a compliment or praise. Share your appreciation with other people. Practice random acts of kindness and expect nothing in return. Put out kindness and positive energy just because you can.

7. See the silver lining in every situation

Ask yourself, "What lesson can I learn from this? How can I avoid this negative event from happening again, or how can I adjust myself and have a different reaction next time?" In every situation, there is opportunity. When something happens, ask yourself,

"Why is this happening *for me*?" instead of thinking it's happening *to you*.

8. Donate

Whether you give of your time, energy, or financial resources, it's very hard to be miserable when you're being generous. Join a foundation that resonates with you because you are grateful for what you are able to earn or what you have been given. Donating helps us live in a place of gratitude because we are helping worthwhile causes and people who are less fortunate.

I like to try and find gratitude in mundane things; instead of complaining that I have to do the laundry, I am grateful that I have an abundance of clothes to wear. Cultivating gratitude doesn't need to be an overly complicated task. Once you get into the hang of it, you will find many things to be grateful for in different aspects of your life.

Here are some examples of inner child gratitude phrases you can build on. Try and list ten things you're grateful for each day.

- *I am grateful that I am alive today.*

- *I am grateful that I discovered my inner child.*

- *I am grateful to be connecting with and healing my inner child.*

- I *am grateful for my inner child.*

- *I am grateful to be healing more and more each day.*

- *I am grateful that I am a strong person.*

- *I am grateful for my past experiences that made me who I am today.*

- *I am grateful for the supportive people in my life.*

Once you get comfortable with the idea of cultivating gratitude, use these prompts to write some of your own gratitude phrases.

I am grateful for _____

I am grateful for _____

I am grateful for _____

If you would like some more examples of simple gratitude phrases, or you would like to be guided through some gratitude exercises, I have an audiobook available on Audible called *Inner Child Healing: Gratitude.*

Wrapping Up Chapter Eight

Self-care and self-love are two more essential tools for your healing journey, and generally, you can't do one without achieving the other. You need to learn to love yourself and your inner child first, and everything else will fall into line. You can reinforce your self-love through affirmations. They are a wonderful way to rewire your brain so that you shift your mindset to a positive one. Another effective way to shift your mindset is by cultivating gratitude for everything you have in life. You are alive, you are strong, and you are going to be okay.

In the next chapter, we will talk about breathwork, how it works, how to do it, and specific breathwork exercises for inner child healing.

CHAPTER NINE:

BREATHWORK

The following breathwork examples are for informational and educational purposes only. They are not intended to be a substitute for professional medical advice or treatment. Always consult a medical professional or healthcare provider if you seek medical advice, diagnoses, and treatment or if you are not sure these are right for you. I am not liable for risks or issues associated with using or acting upon the information provided. Please call a local emergency phone number if you or someone you know is in danger.

What is Breathwork?

Breathwork describes any type of breathing exercise that teaches you to manipulate your breath with different breathing techniques. Breathwork ultimately provides the same benefits that you would get from a meditation practice. You intentionally change your breathing pattern to improve mental, physical, and spiritual health. Although breathwork has become popular in recent years, it has been practiced for centuries by Eastern cultures. The Pranayama breathwork practice dates back to ancient India. Prana means "sacred life force" in Sanskrit. A similar concept is "chi" in traditional Chinese medicine, which describes the "cosmic essence" of breathing. The Japanese use the term "ki" to refer to this concept.

The Benefits of Breathwork

1. Breathwork reduces negative emotions

In today's manic and chaotic world, very few of us haven't experienced depression or anxiety at some point in our lives. Breathwork is a great way to address stress, anxiety, and depression and is an effective method to take control of your moods and emotions so that they don't interfere with your personal life. The way you breathe impacts the way you feel. If you're anxious, you're probably breathing with short rapid breaths, making you feel more stressed and tired. When you're sleeping, you have long, deep breaths that help you feel calm and centered. Deep breathing activates the parasympathetic nervous system, which causes the heart rate to slow down and lowers the blood pressure, creating a feeling of calm. However, beyond just affecting the nervous system, deep breathing also changes your brainwaves. There is a direct correlation between increased alpha brain waves and reduced depression. Breathwork is a great way to shift your brain waves from beta to alpha and even theta, which results in decreased stress, depression, and negative thought patterns.

2. Breathwork boosts the immune system and increases energy levels

Breathwork leads to an increase in oxygen capacity in the blood. This improves your overall energy levels and leaves you with greater stamina. The amount of oxygen you receive through deep breathing directly impacts the amount of energy you have in your cells. Your body can use this extra energy to strengthen your immune system or give you extra energy when you're tired from sleeping poorly the night before.

3. Breathwork increases joy and self-awareness

When doing breathwork exercises, you primarily breathe through your mouth which creates an experience of deep self-awareness. Breathwork gives you the space to go within, where time almost ceases to exist. This is why it's such a wonderful exercise for inner child healing. When your brainwaves change from a state of thinking to more dreamlike, you allow yourself to be in the present moment – to be mindful. As you experience this shift in consciousness, feelings of absolute peace and joy will wash over you.

4. Breathwork increases self-love

Breathwork allows you to shift out of your mind, where you often get stuck in a negative rut, and into your body. An increase in self-love is one of the most direct experiences of breathwork. When you are fully in the experience of breathwork, and your body is vibrating, it is very difficult not to feel a deeper connection with yourself, which cultivates a stronger sense of self-love.

5. Breathwork enhances sleep

With the fast-paced and chaotic world we live in, many of us experience poor sleeping patterns. The good news is that breathwork calms the nervous system, which reduces the effects of environmental stimulants and calms your stress levels, resulting in a better night's sleep.

6. Breathwork allows you to release trapped trauma

Trauma and unprocessed negative emotions can get trapped in the body and block the flow of energy, which often manifests on the physical level. Unresolved trauma and blockages from your childhood hold you back from living the life you desire. Breathwork is a very powerful tool for dislodging and releasing blockages. Breathwork can help you release fear, negative emotions, and limiting beliefs.

7. Breathwork helps reduce pain

It can be all too easy to distance yourself from your body to try and ignore the pain. But breathwork effortlessly connects you with your body, which actually helps you jumpstart the healing process. Deep breathing causes the body to release those happy chemicals called endorphins, which reduce pain sensitivity and boost the sensation of pleasure. Breathwork also helps reduce pain in the body by making the body more alkaline. Breathwork works to reduce cortisol levels, which reduces stress and therefore reduces the feeling of pain. Deep breathing relaxes the muscles that are normally tense due to pain.

8. Breathwork detoxes the blood

Deep breathing detoxifies your blood, promotes a healthy heart, and boosts your lung efficiency. Over fifty percent of toxins in the body are meant to be expelled through your breath, with the main toxin being carbon dioxide. Breathwork expands your diaphragm, relaxing your body and massaging your lymphatic system, which eliminates toxins. Doing breathwork often will help you expel toxins more effectively because your cells are able to take in more oxygen-rich blood.

9. Breathwork improves digestion

Breathwork helps digestion by stimulating and increasing blood flow through the digestive tract. This leads to improved intestinal activity and the reduction of bloating and gas. Breathwork creates a positive loop by reducing stress, which reduces cortisol and reduces gut inflammation.

10. Breathwork alters consciousness

Breathwork is a powerful way to create space for a deeper connection to yourself through spiritual awakening and self-exploration. A breathwork experience can even be compared to something psychedelic and can help you connect to your higher self safely and legally. While doing breathwork, it is not uncommon to experience complete bliss, oneness, and a deep feeling of safety and surrender. It is the perfect place to connect with your inner child. Breathwork affects the way consciousness and unconsciousness work together, which allows you to access your creativity in new ways and gives you more access to the present moment where you can create a new reality.

The Cons of Breathwork

While there are many positive benefits to breathwork, if you're new to the practice or you do it incorrectly, the more challenging techniques may lead to hyperventilation. This can be dangerous because you may also experience:

- Dizziness

- An irregular heartbeat

- Change in vision from lack of oxygen

- Tingling in your hands, arms, feet, or legs

- Muscle spasms

- Ringing in your ears

Deep breathing can also cause chest pain in some cases and may result in breathing difficulties or induce coughing. However, deep breathing and breathwork are not to be confused with big breathing. Breathwork is controlled and deliberate, while big breathing takes in bigger air volumes than necessary. Big breathing leads to over-breathing, affecting the delicate balance of oxygen-carbon dioxide exchange in your body.

Three Breathwork Techniques for Beginners

Please consult with a medical professional about choosing the best method for yourself before trying breathwork.

The 4-7-8 breath for feeling overwhelmed

This is also known as The Relaxing Breath. The 4-7-8 breathing technique slows the body down into a calm and relaxed state. This technique works to slow the heart rate and nervous system, as well as bring you to a place of peace where your consciousness is in the present moment. This breathwork exercise is ideal when you have trouble sleeping, feel triggered, stressed, frustrated, or overwhelmed. We live in a culture where our minds and bodies are inundated with external stimulation, but the 4-7-8 technique teaches the body to take in less, creating a space between the inhale and exhale. It also teaches the body how to release excess energy. This exercise is wonderful for when you are trying to self-soothe after being triggered.

How to do it:

The traditional way of doing the 4-7-8 technique is to empty your lungs of air, inhale through your nose for 4 seconds, hold your breath for 7 seconds and exhale through your mouth for 8 seconds. This should be repeated at least four times.

However, it is about more than just your inhalation and exhalation – it is helpful to get your mind involved as well. As you inhale, visualize the grounding and nurturing energy of the earth, the trees, mountains, and plants coming up into your body. While you're holding your breath, imagine your breath spiraling through the center of your body and pulling out any energy that you do not need. As you exhale, visualize the excess energy expelling from your mouth and imagine a golden white light entering the top of your head and shining all the way down to your feet and into the earth below you.

The 4-4-4-4 breath for when you need a boost

This is also known as Box Breathing or Square Breathing and comes from the Navy SEAL training. This technique works for deepening concentration and slowing down the heart rate. The 4-4-4-4 breathwork technique provides stress relief and increases performance and efficiency. This exercise is best in the morning to get you awake and ready for the day. It can also be used for that afternoon slump, before an activity that requires focus, or during meditation to boost energy.

How to do it:

Begin by emptying all the air from your lungs and then hold your breath for 4 seconds. Inhale for 4 seconds through your nose and hold your breath for another 4 seconds. Then exhale from your nose for 4 seconds. Repeat for at least 5 minutes to feel the effects of this technique.

For the mind part of this exercise, imagine the earth element of the North rising up and sustaining your physical body as you inhale. While you hold your breath, visualize your breath swirling through your mind, like the wind element of the East. Imagine it clearing out any thoughts that no longer serve you. As you exhale, imagine the fire element of the South that makes its home in the heart of your body, burning through the thoughts and emotions that you no longer need and release them from your nose. When you hold your breath again, ask the gentle water element of the West to be with you and guide you through any turbulent waters you may face in life.

The 5-5 breath for when you feel worked up

This technique is also known as the Coherent Breath. We normally breathe at a rate of 2 to 3 seconds per minute, but this technique is all about controlled and conscious breathing that slows the breath down to 4 seconds per minute and then 5 seconds. The 5-5 breath is great for when you're feeling triggered and need to self-soothe. It provides an overall sense of calm and can be practiced whenever you feel like you need it.

How to do it:

Begin by focusing on the rhythm of your natural breath. Then breathe in for 4 seconds, exhale for 4 seconds and do this for a full minute. Repeat by inhaling for 5 seconds and exhaling for 5 seconds and then move up to 6 seconds. If you want to and have the capacity to, gradually expand to 10-second breaths. Begin with a total of 10 minutes and work your way up over time to 20 minutes.

Visualize the earth's energy rising up into your body, and then imagine all the pent-up thoughts, feelings, and physical sensations in your body that you no longer feel the need for, released out of the body through your exhale.

Specific Inner Child Breathwork Technique

This is what Dr. Jim Morningstar had to say about breathwork and inner child healing at the Global Inspiration Conference in Austria in 1997.

"This is all when the "child" part of them is ready to (a) leave the old setting and (b) trust the adult part of them. Breathwork helps ground this in the heart and guts to reorganize their neurology and not just keep it as a nice fantasy. Breathwork surfaces the emotional body more powerfully than verbal or visualization techniques alone and helps integrate the heart and the head. I give assignments to daily consciously breathe and communicate with and listen to their inner child to help build a track record of trust. Also helpful is to have a daily reminder of their intention to heal, such as putting a picture of their inner child or a favorite childhood toy where they will see it regularly. This helps integrate the breathwork into life."

Childhood trauma is stored in the body and results in a wounded inner child. When we don't deal with this trauma, we end up carrying it around with us, and it affects our lives as an adult. There are specific techniques that target the inner child and this stored trauma, including this simple breathwork exercise.

- Begin by sitting in a quiet, comfortable place where you won't be disturbed.

- Take a few deep breaths and bring an unhappy memory that is a source of pain to mind. As uncomfortable as it may be, visualize every detail, the sadness, loneliness, anger, shame, and fear.

● Notice any resistance that comes up in your body. However, if the discomfort from the resistance is too much, it's okay to try again another day.

● Carry on with your breath breathing and repeat affirmations like, "I am safe. I am allowed to feel my emotions."

● Once the uncomfortable feelings from your memory fully encompass you, visualize that you are a force of energy, embodying complete tranquility, peace, security, and love, going back in time to comfort yourself as a child.

● Imagine yourself as a child and become aware of how vulnerable you really were in that moment. Visualize your adult self hovering over your younger self and cover them with a soothing golden-white light. Embrace your younger self and kiss them on the cheek.

● Finally, tell your younger self, "You are worthy. You matter. You are loved." Repeat these affirmations as many times as you feel is needed.

- Take some more deep breaths. On the inhale, breathe in love, acceptance, and healing. On the exhale, breathe out the pain and trauma from the memory.

Wrapping Up Chapter Nine

Deep breathing brings about deep healing. Breathwork is a wonderful tool to add to your inner child healing journey. Not only does breathwork help with the wounded inner child, but it also has an array of other wonderful health benefits that will promote positive overall well-being. If you would like to be guided through the breathwork techniques we went over, I invite you to check out my audiobook available on Audible called *Breathwork for Inner Child Healing*.

In the next chapter, we will cover the basics of meditation, meditation healing, and helpful methods to connect with your inner child.

CHAPTER TEN: MEDITATION HEALING

"Meditation practice isn't about trying to throw ourselves away and become something better, it's about befriending who we are."

Ani Pema Chodron

Over the years, meditation has gained popularity as more people are awakened to its benefits. While some meditation practices originated in Buddhism and Hinduism, meditation is not a fundamentally religious practice. Instead, meditation is about tuning into ourselves to experience being fully present in the moment and cultivating a space of peaceful contemplation. Meditation can be beneficial for many aspects of life, including inner child healing.

What is meditation?

The practice of meditation is just that – a practice. Many people are under the impression that meditation means completely silencing your mind, but that takes years and years of dedicated practice. Meditation can be defined as a set of methods that are meant to encourage a heightened state of awareness and focused attention. In the past, meditation was meant to help a person understand the sacred and complex forces of life. Nowadays, meditation is used for relaxation and reducing stress. Meditation is an alternative form of healing known as mind-body therapy. Meditation takes the focus away from the hundreds of thoughts that crowd our minds that result in stress and promotes a deep state of relaxation that enhances physical and emotional well-being.

12 Benefits of Meditation

Meditation has been shown to thicken the pre-frontal cortex, which is the brain center that manages higher-order brain functions, like concentration, increased awareness, and decision making. With regular meditation, the higher-order functioning part of the brain becomes stronger, while the lower-order brain activities decrease. People use meditation to develop other healthy habits and feelings like a more positive outlook on life, self-discipline, better sleeping patterns, and increased pain tolerance.

Here are 12 science-based benefits of meditation:

1. Reduces Stress

Lowering stress levels is one of the primary reasons people try meditation. Stress increases cortisol levels in the body, which results in the release of inflammatory chemicals as well as causing anxiety and depression, high blood pressure, poor quality sleep, fatigue, and a foggy brain. Research has shown that the symptoms of stress-related conditions can be reduced with regular meditation.

2. Controls Anxiety

This is a direct effect of lower stress levels. Regular meditation also helps with other anxiety-related issues like phobias, social anxiety, and obsessive-compulsive behaviors. A large-scale study concluded that various meditation methods reduce anxiety levels, especially when combined with yoga, because the participants benefited from the meditation and the physical activity.

3. Improved Emotional Health

There are certain methods of meditation that give people a more positive outlook on life which includes a better self-image. One study investigated the electrical activity between people's brains who meditated and those who didn't. The people who meditated had changes in activity relating to areas of the brain associated with optimism and positive thinking.

4. Enhances Self-Awareness

Certain types of meditation help you become more aware of harmful or negative thoughts towards yourself. Meditation develops a stronger sense of self-awareness and understanding yourself. The more self-aware you are, the easier it is to notice your negative thought patterns and create new positive habits.

5. Improved Attention Span

Meditation is a wonderful tool to help increase the strength and endurance of your concentration skills. Meditation has been shown to reverse the brain patterns that result in mind-wandering, foggy brain, worrying and poor attention span. One study showed that even practicing meditation for four days can be enough to positively impact your attention span.

6. Reduced Memory Loss

Improving concentration and clarity of thinking will help keep your mind young and reduce age-related memory loss. The Kirtan Kriya meditation combines chanting or repeating a mantra while your fingers make a repetitive motion which is aimed at controlling the thoughts and increasing the ability to perform memory tasks. Studies have found that meditation increases attention, memory, and mental alertness in older participants. Meditation has also been found to improve the memory of patients with dementia.

7. Generates Kindness

Certain meditation methods, like Metta Meditation (which we will discuss in more detail in the next section), cultivate more positive feelings towards yourself and other people. A study showed that participants who practiced the Metta Meditation had increased feelings of positivity, which reduced household conflict, helped with anger management, and improved social anxiety. Metta Meditation can help create positivity, empathy, and compassion towards others.

8. Fights Addiction

Meditation helps you redirect your attention, increase your awareness about the reason for your behavior, increase willpower and control your emotions and impulses. A study showed that a group of recovering alcoholics who were taught how to meditate could better control their cravings. Meditation helps encourage mental disciplines that break addiction dependencies by increasing self-awareness and self-control.

9. Improves Sleep

Meditation can help you control and redirect the thoughts that often lead to insomnia. Meditation releases tension and shifts you to a peaceful state where your mind and body are more likely to fall asleep. A study investigated the effects of meditation on sleep through two different groups; one group meditated, and the other didn't. The group who meditated fell asleep quicker and slept for longer than the other group.

10. Controls Pain

Pain perception is linked to state of mind, and in stressful situations, pain can be heightened. One study looked at MRI scans to monitor participants' brain activity as they experienced a painful stimulus. Prior to the stimulus, half the group had participated in meditation, and the others had not. The participants who practiced meditation had enhanced activity in the pain control centers of the brain and experienced less pain as a result. In general, meditation results in better pain management and even reduced amounts of pain.

11. Decreases Blood Pressure

Meditation reduces strain on the heart and aids physical health by lowering blood pressure. Meditation controls blood pressure by relaxing nerve signals that work with tension in the blood vessels. This coordinates heart functioning and the flight or fight response in stressful situations.

12. You Can Meditate Anywhere

You don't need a specific space or special equipment to meditate. You also get to choose how long you want to meditate for each day. There are also many different kinds of meditation, so you can choose the one that works for you based on the results you're looking for.

There are two main branches of meditation, and various other methods stem from these:

1. Focused-attention meditation

This type of meditation helps free your mind from the hundreds of thoughts and to-do lists. It focuses on one specific mantra, object, thought, sound, visualization or on the breath.

2. Open-monitoring meditation

This type of meditation helps you become more self-aware by becoming mindful of the thoughts, impulses, and feelings you normally try to suppress. Open-monitoring meditation helps you acknowledge your environment, surroundings, thought patterns, and sense of self.

Choosing a style of meditation to try is very personal, and it's not a case of one-size-fits-all. When I first started meditating, I found myself getting very frustrated in the beginning because I didn't quite understand the point of it. I thought meditating was to sit quietly with a silent mind, so whenever an intruding thought popped into my head, I would feel irritated that I wasn't doing it properly. However, now that I understand what meditation truly is, it is fundamental to my day. Take the time to find a style of meditation that works for you. As your practice grows, you will gradually loosen the restraints of self-centeredness. As you meditate more, your mind will shift to a place where you have a more subtle kind of awareness, and you become less self-conscious and more self-accepting.

Metta Meditation

Meditation is a great way to release trapped emotions within the subconscious. The Metta Meditation practice is also known as loving-kindness meditation. The original name of this meditation *is Metta Bhavana.* Metta means loving-kindness, and Bhavana means cultivation or development. Different cultures and traditions approach meditation differently. However, all forms of Metta Meditation share the same goal, which is to cultivate unconditional positivity towards all beings. The process of developing these emotions is to silently repeat certain phrases that express kind intention toward yourself and other beings. Some examples include:

- May I be healthy in mind and body.

- May I be filled with loving-kindness.

- May you be protected from inner and outer dangers.

The key part of Metta Meditation is reciting the phrases with mindfulness which will help you focus on what you're saying and the emotions associated with it.

Meditation for Inner Child Healing

It is important to remember that our inner child is not separate from who we are and healing the inner child within us is the most important expression of love and compassion toward ourselves. Through this powerful meditation, you can release deep pain and emotional blockages. As you let go of the emotions and heaviness associated with your negative childhood experiences, you will be able to recapture the innocence and joy of your childhood.

A Meditation to Heal Your Inner Child

- Begin by getting into a comfortable position, and relax your body while your mind stays alert.

- Close your eyes. Scan your body and make any adjustments you need to settle into complete comfort.

- Take one big breath in through your nose and exhale through your mouth.

- Carry on breathing and allow yourself to fall deeper into relaxation. Focus on your breath until you feel calm and centered.

- Let your eyelids get heavier.

- Unclench your jaw and relax your cheeks.

- Let go of the tension in your shoulders and relax your arms and hands by your side.

- Soften your chest and stomach and feel your legs and feet get heavier and melt into deeper relaxation.

- Feel your body here in the present moment; soft, warm and relaxed.

- Now begin to imagine yourself as a child and just observe them for a few seconds.

- Look at their hair, their body, their eyes. Notice their position, their attitude, and their expressions. Take this vision of your inner child all in.

- What sounds do you hear them make?

- What scent is around them?

- What is their demeanor?

- Imagine a huge bubble on one side of them – a dark, scary, smokey bubble. As you look closer at the bubble, you recognize what's inside. It's filled with sadness, pain, hurt, and fear. There are so many dark memories inside of this bubble.

- Perhaps you see flashes of those dark memories within it, like mini-movies from your childhood, or maybe you are simply seeing the emotions floating within the bubble and feeling their heaviness.

- This incredible little child has created stories about each one of those emotions or memories. Maybe they created a story called *I'm not good enough, I don't matter, I'm not worthy*, or even *I can't trust others*, or *I can't have everything I want.*

- That little you is not wrong for doing this. It was a way to protect themselves, and it's what all of us do. But these stories they created are not allowing you to live as vibrantly as you would like.

- So take a deep, cleansing breath in through your nose and release the heaviness of these stories as you exhale. Imagine a white piercing light popping this dark bubble. The light surrounds your younger self and envelopes them.

- Now, reach out to this little child and embrace them in your arms, holding them close with pure love. The light surrounds you both.

- Hug them. Love them. Hold them. Accept them. And watch the stories of the past fade away.

- Now, take a step back and observe your younger self again – this beautiful little child.

- A new big, bright bubble surrounds them, and this bubble is filled with laughter, creativity, dreams, and love.

- Perhaps you see flashes of those happy memories within it, like mini-movies from your childhood, or maybe you are simply seeing the emotions floating within it and feeling their lightness – the joy, carefreeness, and imagination.

- Simply sit back and observe it all.
- Feel a smile spread across your face.
- This is all yours, and through this special little child, you can invite more love, more joy, and more creativity into your current life.
- Turn your awareness from this bright bubble onto the little child.
- Can you see how they light up? See how their smile comes from their soul? Remember how much they loved to play? And move? And imagine?
- They are here with you, ready to create more memories of joy to place inside this bubble.
- Stretch your arms out and embrace this gorgeous little child again.
- Feel their pure love saturate you, reminding you that you are them and they are you.
- Bring your attention to your breathing. Feel the hum of peace and calm all over your body.

● *You are so special.*

Sound Frequency

Albert Einstein said it beautifully, "We are slowed down sound and light waves, a walking bundle of frequencies tuned into the cosmos. We are souls dressed up in sacred biochemical garments, and our bodies are the instruments through which our souls play their music."

What is sound frequency healing?

Sound frequency is the foundation and base of all creation, connection, living, and being. Everything physical has some sort of resonance that resonates with the sounds around it, including us. That means that the sounds we listen to have an impact on our body, mind, and soul. Healing frequencies are a form of sound wave therapy that induces a state of ease and harmony in the body. Frequency healing manipulates the brainwaves to promote healing on a physical and spiritual level. Listening to sound frequency is a great method for healing, and listening can be done while meditating or before going to sleep.

Here are three frequencies that are wonderful for healing on the physical, emotional, and spiritual levels.

174hz

174 hertz is one of the Solfeggio frequencies, which are particular sound patterns in the form of frequencies that interact with the brain to generate vibrations within the body, which can induce prominent effects. 174 hertz is associated with relieving pain and stress.

417hz

The 417 hertz is another one of Solfeggio's frequencies and is aimed at removing negative energy on an emotional and spiritual level. This frequency is designed to dissolve emotional blockages (like those caused by past trauma) and activate the sacral chakra.

432hz

According to music theory, the 432 hertz is mathematically consistent with the universe and is known as Verdi's A – named after the famous Italian composer Giuseppe Verdi. This frequency is aimed at the heart chakra and leads to higher levels of emotional and mental clarity. The 432 hertz frequency is associated with higher spiritual development.

Wrapping Up Chapter Ten

Meditation is accessible to everyone and is a practice that everyone can do to improve their physical and mental health, as well as heal their inner child. You can incorporate many other tools into your meditation practice like mantras, mala beads, affirmations, visualization, yoga, tai chi, and frequency healing. If you would like to meditate with healing frequencies, I have a 432 HZ healing sound frequency meditation for inner child healing on Audible called *Guided Meditation for Inner Child Healing.*

In the next chapter, we will discuss the power of journaling to heal your wounded inner child.

CHAPTER ELEVEN: THE MIGHTY PEN

"Writing is medicine. It is an
appropriate antidote to injury. It is an
appropriate companion for any
difficult change."

Julia Cameron

While it might seem counterintuitive, writing about the negative experiences of the past has a positive effect on our adult self. Emotional writing about past experiences and ongoing anxiety frees up our cognitive resources, so we are better able to focus on healing. Research has shown that trauma damages the tissue in the brain, but when we translate our experiences into words, we are changing the way the trauma is organized in the brain.

The Seven Benefits of Writing

As insignificant as it may seem, writing your thoughts, feelings, worries, and emotions down has scientifically proven benefits that can help you turn the chaos of your mind into the most basic sense.

Here are seven benefits of writing things down:

1. **Writing serves as a record for thoughts that have your attention**

In the day and age we live in, we are constantly bombarded with tasks we need to do and things we need to remember. Our plates are overflowing, and feeling the need to be on top of things leaves us feeling overwhelmed and exhausted. By writing things down, you can record anything and everything that is taking up your attention. Once it's down on paper, you have access to these things whenever it is necessary.

2. Writing clears the mind

Once you've picked up a pen and paper or even opened the notes on your phone and written everything down, you will experience a sense of relief. Even if you don't tick anything off your list, there is a short period of transformation where your brain has a moment of silence away from the pesky thoughts, and the first stages of organization can begin.

3. Writing clarifies your goals, intentions, and priorities

When you write down your goals, intentions, and priorities, you are forced to literally see and assess each one of them. They are no longer a pie-in-the-sky notion but an almost-tangible reality.

4. Writing keeps you motivated

It doesn't matter if you're a superhuman or not; motivation doesn't last forever. It's easy to feel bursts of excitement and energy, but even with the strongest and most relevant goals, we tend to fall back into a place where we lack motivation. By writing things down, you can keep your attention on your goals and remind yourself about your purpose on a regular basis.

5. Writing helps with recognizing and processing emotions

The manic lives we live lead to elevated stress, anxiety, and even serious health problems. Stress is one of the leading causes of disease. Thankfully, writing can significantly reduce stress and anxiety. When you put your emotions into words on a piece of paper, you are able to process your thoughts on a much deeper level. Writing gives you a bit of a third-person perspective which helps you organize and deal with your emotions. Writing is also a form of release therapy for whenever you're feeling triggered.

6. Writing encourages daily progress

Before we try to become better people by improving ourselves, our actions, and our thoughts, we need to assess our past and current situation. Writing helps us compile a record of what we've experienced, thought, felt, and acted on so we can reflect on what has worked and what hasn't. Through writing, we can gauge our strengths and weaknesses to move forward in the right way.

7. Writing enables higher thinking and focused action

When our brains are not trying to remember every single thing, they can process a lot more. When we're feeling overwhelmed, it's difficult to analyze the situation and ask the important questions. By writing everything down, you give your brain the chance to focus on what's actually important, what you need to prioritize and take action towards.

What is journaling?

Journaling is a wonderful technique for inner child healing. It is a written account of your thoughts and feelings as you experience everyday life. The wonderful thing about journaling is that there is no wrong or right way to do it. It is an extremely personal experience, and you need to journal in the way that resonates with you the most. One day, your journaling could look like a diary entry like the one you used to write when you were a teenager. The next day it could be a list of your gratitudes or the goals you want to achieve.

Cultivating a habit of journaling will help you work through any emotions you're experiencing, especially if you're feeling anxious or upset. Journaling helps you become more self-aware, helps you grow, and helps you gain more meaningful insights. Journaling is considered to be one of the best self-improvement tools.

The Benefits of Journaling

Whether you're using your journal to work through childhood trauma, heal your inner child or deal with the stress of your current life, this activity has many benefits, including:

- Managing anxiety.

- Reducing stress levels.

- Coping with depression.

- Prioritizing problems and fears.

- Tracking your problems to see what triggers you and how to be more aware to solve them more effectively.

- Identifying negative thoughts and behaviors.

- Clarifying your thoughts and feelings to become more self-aware.

- Allowing you to see your problems with more clarity and putting a different perspective on the things happening in your life.

- Allowing you to work through difficult experiences in your past.

- Helping you connect and communicate with your inner child to bring about healing.

How to journal

As I mentioned previously, journaling is a deeply personal experience. I am a fan of a good old-fashioned notebook and pen, but you need to find a journaling style that works for you.

Here are some of the basic steps to begin your journaling journey:

1. Find the technique that resonates with you

Many people share my sentiment regarding pen and paper because it helps them focus on the activity at hand and express their ideas more clearly without being interrupted by social media notifications or emails. However, a pen and notebook aren't the only ways to journal, and you may prefer using a laptop or your phone. It's all about finding the method that works best for you.

2. Let go of all judgment

Journaling is for your eyes only, and there is no right or wrong way to do it. You can use journaling as a way to leave your inner critic behind and practice self-compassion.

3. Manage your expectations

When you begin journaling, don't expect to write pages and pages filled with insightful thoughts. If your expectations are unrealistic, you may end up feeling discouraged. Remember that journaling is a practice, and you need to build the habit using baby steps.

4. Create a routine

It's easy to journal on days when you're feeling motivated and inspired, but that's not what it's all about. Creating a writing routine will help you schedule in time to journal, which will keep you on track for those days when you're feeling uninspired.

5. Journal about anything that comes to mind

The possibilities are limitless when it comes to journaling. You can write about your day, emotions, something that's bugging you, goals, or something that inspired you. You can use journaling as an outlet to release your heavy emotions so that you can gain clarity and let them go. You can use your journal to explore past experiences that impacted you as a child so that you can work through them.

6. Use journal prompts

There will be days when you pick up your journal and have no idea what to write about. That is where journal prompts are handy. There are hundreds of journal prompts available online to get you inspired. Print some out and keep them in the back of your journal for when you hit a blank. Some of my favorite prompts for inner child healing include:

- *Explain a time as a child when you felt misunderstood or neglected. What do you wish you could say now? Take a moment to check in with your inner child to see how they want to be nurtured in this situation.*

○ *If you could just tell your inner child one thing, what would you say to them and why?*

○ *Describe a quality that you had as a little one that you loved and wished you still had now.*

7. Get creative

Your journal is a way for you to express yourself, whether that be through words, poetry, lyrics, sketching, or art. It is for anything that allows you to express your emotions, thoughts and feelings.

Journal As Your Inner Child

Journaling can help you recognize patterns and behaviors in your life that you want to change as an adult. However, journaling from the perspective of your inner child can help you see which unhelpful patterns originated from your childhood.

For this journaling exercise, try a meditation or visualization technique that allows you to connect with your inner child at the specific age you want to explore. Set your adult self aside and let your inner child take front and center. Once you're connected and in the right mindset, write down some of the memories and emotions you associate with the event at hand. Don't overthink this – just start writing and let your thoughts flow onto the paper as they enter your mind. Expressing yourself in an unhindered way will help you get to the root of your inner child's pain.

Write a Letter to Your Inner Child

Writing a letter to your inner child is another wonderful way to connect with them and open the door for healing. There is no specific way to do this – you just need to write whatever comes to your heart. You might address certain memories from your childhood and offer insight or explanation for experiences you did not understand back then. Maybe you never understood why your father always took your toys or shouted at you, but you learned to fear him because of it. Since then, you have come to realize that he experienced years of abuse and bullying, and his behavior has begun to make sense. You can share this new insight with your inner child through your letter to help soothe that lingering confusion and suffering.

Writing a letter to your inner child will give you the chance to send them messages of nurturing support and reassurance. Mulling over certain questions will eventually lead to answers, although it may take some time before your inner child feels comforted and secure, so be patient.

Some questions to ask to get the dialogue going include:

- How are you feeling?

- What can I do to support you?

- What do you need from me right now?

Writing a letter to your inner child or *emotional writing* about your childhood memories will help you explore your past experiences and deal with the associated emotions. It is completely normal to feel nervous about what your inner child has to say, especially if you have buried difficult emotions and negative childhood experiences. But remember that this exercise is a way to establish and strengthen the bond between your adult self and the little one inside of you.

More Journal Prompts for Inner Child Healing

- What activities did you enjoy as a child? Why did you stop doing them? Would you like to do them again? Why or why not?

- What was your favorite game as a child? Did you have imaginary friends? What was their energy like?

- Who hurt you the most as a child? Are you able to forgive them now? Why or why not?

- Write about a time when you felt like you lost your "childhood innocence."

- How can you nurture and comfort your inner child now?

- Write about an experience in your childhood that made you feel insecure and not good enough. These experiences are what started self-limiting beliefs. Ask your inner child what you can do now to release these beliefs.

Wrapping Up Chapter Eleven

Writing is a very powerful tool. Your journal is a non-judgmental place where you can express yourself – the joy and the pain. Journaling is a way to journey inside, a way for you to meet with your inner child and provide them with reassurance and healing. If you would like to explore journaling in more depth using a guided audio to listen to and follow along with, I have an audiobook available on Audible called "Powerful Journaling for Inner Child Healing."

The next chapter will cover how to release your inner artist and how art therapy can help heal your inner child.

CHAPTER TWELVE: BACK TO THE DRAWING BOARD

"Creating artwork allows your mind to be in a safe place while it contemplates the tougher issues you are dealing with. One can use the tools of brush, paint, pastels, crayons, etc., to expose and even for a short time color those issues in a different light."

George E. Miller

Oscar Wilde once said, "Man is least himself when he talks in his own person. Give him a mask, and he will tell you the truth." Art provides us with a way to communicate our experiences when words are insufficient. Humans use artistic expression as a way to adapt to challenges and trauma. Art therapy is a fantastic way to engage our creativity and induce our imagination. It allows us to transform the complexities of adulthood while healing our inner child. One form of art therapy that really allows us to connect with our inner child is *inner child drawings*. Art is a profound way to access the aspects of our psyche that we don't normally pay attention to.

What Is Art Therapy?

The use of artistic methods to treat trauma, psychological disorders, and mental health is known as art therapy. It is a technique grounded in the idea that creative expression fosters healing and emotional well-being. The well-known saying, "A picture is worth a thousand words," reinforces the powerful effect of art and creative expression on our human communication and understanding. Art therapy works to harness that power for healing.

Licensed professionals are trained in both art and therapy to carry out these sessions. Art therapy is suitable for people of any age. One of the primary goals of art therapy is to improve people's well-being to bring about deep, soulful healing. You do not need to worry about being an artist or even being "good at art" to benefit from art therapy. This form of therapy is not just about attending an art class or keeping yourself preoccupied. It's about using the power of art and creative expression to help you open up and understand yourself in new ways, which will enhance healing of all kinds.

How Does Art Therapy Work?

People who partake in art therapy of any form, whether they consider themselves an artist or not, are partaking in the process of self-discovery. This journey gives you a safe space to express your feelings and it allows you to feel more in control over your life. Art therapy can take place in many different forms, including painting, drawing, finger painting, working with clay, carving, sculpting, doodling and scribbling, or making collages. Through these integrative methods, art therapy allows you to engage your mind, body, and spirit in ways that are very different from verbal therapy alone. The sensory, perceptual, symbolic, and kinesthetic opportunities invite a deeper understanding of yourself and the ability to communicate expressively without having to rely on words alone.

Benefits Of Art Therapy

According to a 2016 study published in the Journal of the American Art Therapy Association, just one hour of creative activity positively affects our mental health and majorly reduces our stress levels (regardless of talent or artistic experience). People who have experienced abuse, neglect, emotional trauma, violence, depression, anxiety, and other psychological issues can benefit from expressing themselves creatively. Art therapy benefits people of all ages. Research has shown that art therapy is a useful tool for concentration and communication and helps to reduce feelings of isolation and loneliness. Art therapy has also been shown to lead to an increase in confidence, self-esteem, and self-awareness. Aside from all of these benefits, art therapy is also just a wonderful way to feel like a kid again and, in turn, heal your inner child.

Inner Child Drawings

Inner child drawings are a form of art therapy that uses a creative method to connect with aspects of your psyche that you may otherwise suppress or ignore. Typically, inner child drawings are done with the non-dominant hand. This is so that you're not tempted to try and control them with your authoritarian left brain. It is also great to buy yourself a box of kid's crayons or colored pencils to support your inner child's creative process.

Artist Heather Williams, the author of *Drawing as a Sacred Activity*, has an exceptional exercise[i] to help you access your inner child. You can challenge yourself by trying out this process for thirty days.

Inner Child Drawing Challenge

What you need to get started:

- Number your sketchbook pages from 1 to 30.

- Each day, for thirty days, create a spontaneous drawing.

● Make notes of any insights that arise while doing this.

Daily Inner Child Drawing Exercise

1. Begin by relaxing and taking a few deep breaths. Have your paper and crayons or pencils in front of you.

2. Close your eyes and connect with your inner child. Visualize or feel a child near you. Notice the color of their hair, height, posture, and clothing. Open your heart and feel yourself accepting this child exactly as they are, even if the child is angry, sad, or frightened. Then, draw a picture of your inner child at that moment with your non-dominant hand.

3. Ask this child to play a game with you. As the adult, ask the child these questions. Write the questions on the top or bottom of your drawing in your dominant hand.

   ○ What is your name?

   ○ How old are you?

   ○ What are you feeling right now?

o   What can I do to help you feel safe and happy?

4. Then, let your inner child draw a picture of itself for you and answer the questions using your crayons or colored pencils. Draw and answer the questions with your non-dominant hand.

5.   Thank your inner child for sharing with you, and take a moment to reflect on anything that may have come to light.

Keep in mind that as you draw for thirty days in a row, you may witness many different inner children surfacing to gain your attention. Some of the children will be happy, some will be angry, and others will be sad. Some of these children may have been buried and repressed, and others are barely alive because of lack of attention. You need to compassionately allow all of them to have their full expression, no matter how childish they may seem. Prepare yourself for fear and suppressed feelings to come up during this activity. But also expect a great sense of relief, inner excitement, and joy. The younger, exiled parts of your personality long to be heard and will gladly share their truth through your non-dominant hand.

Guidelines for the Best Self-Expression of Your Inner Child Through Art Therapy

It is important to treat your inner child as you would a real child. Be compassionate, comforting, gentle, and show genuine interest. In essence, the activity of inner child drawing allows your dominant hand to parent and nurture your inner child through your non-dominant hand.

The following guidelines are inspired by Michele Cassou, author of Kid's Play.

- Always approach creativity as a process-oriented activity, and don't ever expect your inner child to draw perfectly.

- Never ask your inner child to paint or draw realistically.

- Never tell your inner child what to draw or paint, and don't give them something to copy either.

- Never correct your inner child's drawing, and don't ask them to fix anything.

- Never criticize or praise your inner child's drawing. Simply observe them with acceptance.

- Never ask your inner child what their drawings represent or why they painted or drew them. Create a safe, non-judgmental environment for the free and non-intrusive expression of their feelings through imagery.

- Show care, respect, and interest for everything your inner child creates.

- Observe your inner child's process with understanding and interest. It is important that they feel seen.

- Never compare your inner child's work and never encourage competition.

- When your inner child asks for help to draw or paint, don't show them exactly how to. Rather encourage them and help them realize they can create anything they want.

- Appreciate your inner child for who they are and how they feel, not what they do.

"We nurture our creativity when we release our inner child."

Serina Hartwell

Wrapping Up Chapter Twelve

Art is not always about pretty things. It is about who we are, what happened to us, and how our lives are affected. Art therapy is any form of creative expression, and with that expression comes transformation. This creative expression can take the form of many different activities and is not only limited to drawing. You can try painting, sculpting, collaging, doodling, or coloring. If you find that art therapy just isn't for you, I encourage you to look into other forms of creative therapy where you can express yourself, including drama therapy, dance therapy, music therapy, writing therapy, or expressive therapy.

If you would like to explore art therapy through coloring, I have a coloring book available on Amazon called *Coloring for Inner Child Healing*, filled with colorable designs and affirmations for inner child healing.

In the next and final chapter, we will cover communicating with others, where we will look at tips and tricks on how to communicate with someone about how your inner child is feeling.

CHAPTER THIRTEEN: COMMUNICATION WITH OTHERS

Communicate. Even when it's uncomfortable or uneasy. One of the best ways to heal is simply getting everything out.

Unknown

Your inner child is the house of unmet needs and childhood traumas embedded in your unconscious mind. The process of healing and connecting with your inner child may trigger emotions from the deep wounds of your childhood. Often, we may feel overwhelmed by our emotions, and it is at this moment, that our inner child and the deep wounds are being touched, which causes the trigger. When we are in this state of reactivity, and we try to communicate with our family, friends, or partner, we tend to lead with "other" based language – we use the word *you*. We say things like. You *said, you did, you always do.* And when we use language like that, the other person (who is supposed to be listening) often begins to feel threatened. It is human instinct to hear something directed at us through the word *you* and get our backs up. The nervous system is triggered, and we perceive what comes next as a threat. When humans feel threatened, they don't listen. But don't be discouraged. It is still important to share these feelings with the people in your life who care about you and want to support you – there is just a certain way to go about doing it. Communicating is easiest when you're in a safe space so you can set yourself up to be heard.

The bottom line is we want to avoid the type of language that involves blame, so when we share our feelings and the feelings our inner child may be having, we are heard. We want to evolve our relationships into safe spaces for communication, especially when our words and deep feelings are coming to the surface.

This is how you can shift your words to feel safer, heard, and recognized by the people around you.

1. The first step is to practice beginning with "my inner child is feeling" instead of "you." The shift from *you* to *my inner child* allows the listener to rest and feel safe, be more receptive, and hear what's coming next instead of their senses becoming activated and shutting down to what you have to say. This will feel more comfortable with practice and will go a long way to ensure your feelings are heard.

2. The second step is to take a moment and pause. Sharing your feelings this way may feel weird because it's not normally how you talk, and strong emotions may come up. You want to pause and allow these feelings and emotions to wash over you. You may feel vulnerable and surprised by the things coming to the surface, but when you pause, you allow the feelings to be released. This can be physical in the form of an energetic release like bodily sensations or tears. Many of us have had these energies and fears contained and stuck in our bodies, so

taking a moment to just feel will allow the energetic blockages to be released.

3. The third step is to allow the other person to have time to process their feelings around what you just shared. The time may vary depending from person to person. Some people can process and be in the moment in real-time. Other people may take hours or days. Just allow the person to sit with their feelings regarding what you just shared. Have the patience to allow the listener to have their space to process.

4. The final step is to actively listen. Once the person has had time to sit and process, they might want to share their feelings based on what they've heard from you. Practice active listening. Allow the person to respond in the same way they allowed you to share, creating safety and learning to practice hearing how someone else feels.

This is a practice and process and doesn't happen overnight. It is challenging to share your feelings with others. But we want to learn to evolve our relationships into safer spaces, and these tips are a good way to begin.

Professional Help

Sometimes, to fully heal a deeply wounded inner child, you may need to see a professional therapist to relive and re-experience your childhood traumas. Only then can you go on to take care of and heal your wounded inner child. Everyone is different and may require a different method of healing. If you find that none of the holistic healing methods work for you, other forms of therapy with licensed professionals may be more comforting and beneficial to the journey of healing your inner child.

These include:

1. **Eye Movement Desensitization and Reprocessing (EMDR)**

    EMDR therapy focuses directly on the memory. It is intended to change how the memory is stored in the brain, which reduces and eliminates problematic symptoms and trauma.

2. Neuro-linguistic Programming (NLP)

NLP therapy is a psychological approach involving analyzing strategies used by successful individuals and applying them to reach personal goals. NLP relates language, thoughts, and behavior patterns learned through experiences to specific outcomes.

3. Gestalt

Gestalt therapy is used to teach people how to become aware of significant sensations within their environment and themselves so that they can respond fully and reasonably to situations.

4. Hypnotherapy

Hypnotherapy takes place through a guided session where the patient is induced into a trance-like state that helps them become deeply relaxed, focus their mind, and respond more readily to suggestions. Hypnotherapy uses the heightened awareness of the hypnotic state to help the person focus on a problem in more depth.

5. Personal Development Classes

Personal development classes may include anything from improving self-awareness, improving self-knowledge, or improving skills and learning new ones.

6. Cognitive Behavioral Therapy (CBT)

CBT is a form of psychological therapy used on a range of issues like addiction, trauma, mental illness, stress, anxiety, and depression. In CBT, negative thought patterns about oneself and the world are challenged in order to alter unwanted behavioral patterns or treat mood disorders.

I encourage you to explore some of these therapies in more depth if any of them resonate with you or you feel that you need the help of a professional – and remember that it is completely okay.

Wrapping Up Chapter Thirteen

While it may be scary to share the emotions of your inner child with others, it is a very important part of the healing journey. Communicating with the people in your life in an honest, sincere, and gentle way will help build stronger, better, and healthier relationships.

Leave A Review

If you found this book helpful for your healing journey, please leave a 1- click review so that others who are looking to discover and/or heal their inner child can find my book too.

I would be incredibly grateful and thankful if you could take 60 seconds to leave a review of your honest feedback, even if it's just a few sentences.

Thank you kindly.

-Caldwell Ramsey

Customer reviews

5 star		0%
4 star		0%
3 star		0%
2 star		0%
1 star		0%

˅ How customer reviews and ratings work

Review this product

Share your thoughts with other customers

Write a customer review

Conclusion

Sitting in a corner
Huddled in the dark
I found her sobbing
in anguish stark;

A child was she
Not more than six
Her broken heart
I longed to fix.

Approaching her gently
I knelt, sat down;
But instead of smiling
Looking up, she frowned.

"What do you want?
Go away," she said
Her moist eyes glared
A fiery-red.

"I'm here for you
your confidante
you can trust me."

"No, I possibly can't...
... I've been let down
Hurt, shamed, betrayed
I feel worthless
Unloved, disgraced...
... Where were you when
they gave me pain
Misunderstood me
Poured all the blame?"

"Asleep," said I
"unsure and lost
till the guide within
revealed true north...
... It's been a long way
Till finally today
Behind an old door
I saw you there.
Look closely in
my eyes, you'll see:
A grown-up version
Of yourself — it's me!"

Hearing this, she
hugged me tight

she sobbed and sobbed
till her heart was light.

Since then, she laughs
and plays in the sun
feels safe and loved
Knowing we are one.

The Inner Child Poem

Thank you for trusting me enough to make it to the end of this book. I am so honored that I was able to share my journey of healing with you. After discovering that my inner child was wounded and experiencing the relief that came with healing them, I knew that I needed to help others navigate this trauma. This book is the labor of love, born from my own pain and experience. I felt that it was my mission to provide insight and the necessary tools to help people find inner child healing, especially in their darkest moments.

You reach a point in your life where you have to make a choice; you can either carry along down the slippery slope you're on, or you can choose to heal. I remember what it was like to suffer from emotional pain, stress, anxiety, and self-sabotaging tendencies and not even realize that it was my inner child trying to call out to me. The negative patterns in my life resulted from my wounded inner child. My hope is that after finishing this book, you are aware of the power of inner child healing and are equipped with the necessary tools and healing methods to heal your own wounded inner child.

I hope that once you've worked through the techniques in this book, you will have a deeper understanding of the trauma you experienced as a child and how it's affecting you as an adult. You may feel like you're stuck in a toxic rut, but the methods in this book are there to guide you through the healing journey. It won't always be easy, but it will be worth it. The freedom that comes with healing the wounded child within is like no other.

Keep this book close for when you are feeling lost, alone, and in need of a guiding light. This book is something to lean on, a beacon of hope for when you feel like the waves are getting too rough. Remember the words of advice I've written from the depths of my heart and follow them to the best of your ability. I believe in you, and I know you will make it through and come out a completely new person in the end. You may have a more grown-up body and more life experience, but you are every bit as precious. Love yourself as if you were the most precious thing in the world – because you are!

Here is a quick recap of the main topics we covered throughout this book to remind you how much you have learned since we started this journey together.

Although your inner child is not physical or tangible, it is part of your deep subconscious. It has been with you since the day you were born, always absorbing everything around you, including trauma you may have experienced in your childhood. As an adult, you are probably trying to run away from your inner child, or at least the pain inside. You don't want to face those feelings again, and as a result, you end up suppressing your inner child, which ends up wreaking havoc in your adult life. Being detached from your inner child is a lot more common than people realize, and having a wounded inner child is something many adults struggle with. In order to truly heal, you have to acknowledge, embrace and nurture the child within, making them feel safe and protected again. You have to face the trauma or painful experiences from your childhood so that you can set yourself free once and for all.

Childhood trauma leads to adults living in survival mode, too afraid to plant roots, plan for the future, trust others, and let joy in. Trauma causes more than just an emotional response; it affects the brain on a cellular level, which continues to impact your life today. Stress is a common part of life but experiencing toxic stress as a child leads to damaging long-term effects. Trauma and stress affect the parts of the brain linked with memory, emotions, sensory processing, memory, and learning. Trauma can lead to difficulties regulating emotions, chronic stress, difficulty concentrating and learning, and feeling permanently anxious, fearful, and irritated. Childhood trauma can result in many psychological issues, and some adults even suffer from PTSD. Adults who suffer from childhood trauma and toxic stress experience significant consequences on an emotional, physical and mental level. Fortunately, you can heal yourself.

However, healing begins with deciding that you want to heal. You are the only one who can heal yourself, and you must make the conscious decision to do exactly that. Healing is hard work, but it's necessary work. When you embark on this journey to heal your inner child, you need to treat yourself like you would treat someone you held dearly to your heart. You need to have compassion and understanding and approach your healing from a place of zero judgment. It is important to cultivate a healing mindset that will carry you through this journey. Your brain has the ability to change with repetition, which is known as neuroplasticity. Repetitive behaviors grow and alter your brain matter, regardless of how old you are. This also refers to positive thinking and a healing mindset. The more consistent your positive thoughts are, the more the brain neurons change their chemical signals, which adapt the functioning and structure of the brain associated with positive behavioral changes and healing.

Your subconscious mind remembers everything, even if you don't, and as you grow up, your inner child doesn't just disappear. When you are triggered by seemingly insignificant situations and don't understand why, it's because the inner child inside of you is still there and screaming for attention. Your inner child is wounded and needs to be healed, not suppressed and ignored. Inner child healing is a way for you to acknowledge and embrace your inner child as a separate person. It is a way for you to make it known that your intention is to heal their wounds. Inner child healing is so important because, on a psychological level, a wounded inner child could be the underlying cause behind low self-esteem, depression, anger, self-sabotage, abandonment issues, or relationship difficulties you're facing. Healing your childhood traumas will help you live a wonderful, fulfilled life now in the present moment. Another aspect of inner child healing is the realization that your parents may not have been able to meet your needs because they didn't even know how to meet their own. It's okay to feel angry at the parents your inner child was raised by, but it's also essential to remember that the wound may not have been your fault, but the healing is your responsibility.

Even if you can happily report that you enjoyed a wonderful childhood, they are likely trauma or experiences that hurt you and impact how you view the world. Fortunately, there is a way to overcome any beliefs or baggage you carry around. And one of those ways is through reparenting. Simply put, reparenting is the act of giving yourself what you didn't receive as a child. As an adult, it's impossible to return to your childhood, so you need to reparent as a way to give yourself what was missing from your first years of life. Reparenting is your own personal responsibility and begins with asking yourself, *"What do I need? What can I do for myself today?"* There are four key pillars to reparenting; emotional regulation, loving discipline, self-care, and joy. Depending on your unique childhood trauma and experiences, some of these pillars could be more challenging than others.

The next important step in your inner child healing journal is the energy of mindfulness. Mindfulness is one of the ways through to your inner child. It is the energy that helps you to be entirely present so that you can connect with your inner child on a different level. At its core, mindfulness is a practice that needs to be repeated regularly and with intention. You need to incorporate mindfulness into your daily routine to cultivate a space for yourself and your inner child. The five steps for putting mindfulness into practice are starting your day with a mindful morning, eating your food mindfully, rewiring your brain by pausing, activating your mind and your muscles, and driving your car mindfully. Another way to cultivate mindfulness is through a body scan meditation.

Validating and noticing yourself as well as your inner child is essential for inner child healing. Self-validation is a skill that takes practice, and at first, it won't be easy, especially if you never received much validation as a child. Some important lists to create during the process of validating and noticing yourself are a list of your needs, a list of things that make you feel nurtured, and a list of boundaries. Having a list of your needs will serve as a helpful reminder as well as help you reinforce the boundaries needed to protect your inner child. The second list is one of comforting phrases that you can repeat to yourself when you are feeling triggered. The final list is one of healthy boundaries that you need for a happy life. Boundaries result from understanding your needs and using your voice to bring them to light.

Beyond noticing and validating yourself, you also need to focus on self-love and self-care. While you're on the journey to healing your inner child, you still need to nurture and look after your current adult self. Self-care is being conscious of your own needs, physically, emotionally, and mentally and ensuring that they are met. Self-love is accepting yourself completely, treating yourself with kindness and respect, and nurturing your growth and wellbeing. Affirmations are a great way to reiterate self-care and self-love and rewire your brain positively. Affirmations are carefully constructed to have the most impact and can help you challenge and overcome self-sabotaging and negative thoughts. Gratitude is another key part of personal healing. An attitude of gratitude can be cultivated and used to help you appreciate things on a deeper level. It helps you relish good experiences and feel more positive emotions.

Another very useful tool for inner child healing is breathwork. Proper breathing is so important for your overall wellbeing. There are many benefits to practicing breathwork, like reducing negative emotions, boosting your immune system, increasing self-awareness and joy, increasing self-love, enhancing sleep, reducing trapped trauma, and altering your consciousness. Some simple breathwork techniques to start with include the 4-7-8 breath, the 4-4-4-4 breath, and the 5-5 breath.

Breathwork can be practiced alongside meditation, a powerful healing method for inner child healing.

Meditation has been shown to thicken the pre-frontal cortex, which is the brain center that manages higher-order brain functions, like concentration, increased awareness, and decision making. Meditation has many benefits, including reducing stress, improving emotional wellbeing, enhancing self-awareness, reducing memory loss, increasing attention span, generating kindness, improving sleep, fighting addiction, controlling pain, and healing the inner child. Meditation can be used to connect with your inner child and release deep and painful emotional blockages.

Another very useful tool for inner child healing is the power of writing. Emotional writing about past experiences and ongoing anxiety frees up your cognitive resources, so you can better focus on healing your inner child. Journaling is a wonderful writing technique you can incorporate into your daily routine to bring about deep healing. There is no wrong or right way to journal; it is simply about finding a method that works for you. Journaling can help you recognize patterns and behaviors in your life that you want to change as an adult, but it can also help you understand where those behaviors originated from in childhood so that you can work to overcome them. Another helpful writing technique includes writing a letter to your inner child. You can address certain memories from your childhood, provide them with clarity surrounding an experience, or write about anything else you feel is needed. Emotional writing is all about creative expression, and there is no place for judgment.

Another form of creative expression is art therapy. Whether you're "good" at art or not, this form of therapy has many benefits. Art allows you to transform the complexities of adulthood while healing your inner child. It is a way for you to connect with your inner child and express your feelings when words are not enough. Art therapy allows you to engage your mind, body, and spirit in ways that are very different from verbal therapy alone. One of the beneficial exercises of art therapy includes inner child drawings. These are a great way for you to connect with your inner child and express your feelings.

The final part of inner child healing is learning to communicate with others about what your inner child is feeling. When you speak to the people closest to you about your feelings, you want to avoid the type of language that involves blame. It is all about approaching them in the right manner, sharing your story, and allowing them the space to think about what you've said. Communication takes practice, but it is essential for building stronger, more supportive relationships.

Now that you know the different methods to begin connecting with and healing your inner child, I hope you are ready to start your journey to becoming a healed, authentic version of yourself, living with deep inner freedom. Please remember that you are never alone. There is always support. You just need to ask for it and allow the healing to take place. Healing takes time, and the road may be rocky, but it is definitely worth it. I wish you nothing but happiness and joy on your healing journey.

If you enjoyed this book, please feel free to leave a review on Amazon so that other people looking for ways to heal their inner child can find the book and discover inner child healing for themselves. Having a healed inner child is an amazing gift we can give ourselves and ultimately the world because that love is extended to everyone.

Find More on Audible!

Search: Caldwell Ramsey

- <u>Powerful Journaling for Inner Child Healing</u> : Guided Prompts for Your Journey to Recovery of Wounds and Past Trauma. Enhance Meditation, Inner Work, and Therapy.

- <u>Breathwork for Inner Child Healing</u> : Guided Techniques to Complement Inner Work, Relieve Stress, and Triggers. Free Yourself from Past Trauma and Heal from Within.

- <u>Daily Gratitude: Inner Child Healing</u> : A Guided Gratitude List of 300+ Things to Be Grateful for During Your Journey to Recovery of Past Trauma and Wounds

- <u>Guided Meditation for Inner Child Healing</u> : A Powerful Connection with Your Inner Child to Reparent, Heal Wounds, and Unchain Yourself from Childhood Trauma

- <u>200+ Powerful Affirmations for Your Inner Child</u> : Heal Deep Wounds and Free Yourself from Past Trauma. Enhance Meditation, Inner Work, and Therapy.

- <u>Inner Child Healing: Self Affirmations</u> : Heal Deep Wounds and Free Yourself from Past Trauma. Enhance Meditation, Inner Work, and Therapy.

- <u>Rebirth Meditation for Inner Child Healing:</u> A Guided Meditation to be Reborn, Free Yourself from Limiting Beliefs and Childhood Trauma. Enhance Inner Child Work, Shadow Work, Therapy and Reparenting.

- <u>Ultimate 3-in-1 Daily Inner Child Healing Bundle</u> : Includes Three Daily Exercises Specifically for Your Inner Child Healing Journey: Daily Gratitude, Self-Affirmations, Affirmations for Your Inner Child

- <u>Powerful 3-in-1 Deep Dive Inner Child Healing Bundle</u> : Includes Three Powerful Exercises Specifically for Your Inner Child Healing Journey: Guided Meditation, 22 Journaling Prompts, Guided Breathwork

Just For You

A Free Gift For All

My Readers

Inner Child Healing Workbook with complementary tools for your healing journey. Visit my website:

www.CaldwellRamseybooks.com

Resources

1. https://www.samhsa.gov/child-trauma/understanding-child-trauma#:~:text=At%20least%201%20in%207,for%20physical%20assault-related%20injuries

2. https://med.stanford.edu/news/all-news/2017/03/health-care-providers-should-harness-power-of-mindsets.html

3. https://www.expressiveartworkshops.com/expressive-art-e-courses/30-day-expressive-drawing-challenges/inner-child-drawings/